TELL

Women's Devotional

Janice Rigel

Published by KHARIS PUBLISHING, an imprint of KHARIS MEDIA
LLC.

Copyright © 2023 Janice Rigel

ISBN-13: 978-1-63746-200-3

ISBN-10: 1-63746-200-X

Library of Congress Control Number: 2022951269

All KHARIS PUBLISHING products are available at special quantity
discounts for bulk purchases for sales promotions, premiums, fund-raising,
and educational needs. For details, contact:

Kharis Media LLC
Tel: 1-479-599-8657
support@kharispublishing.com
www.kharispublishing.com

BOOK DEDICATION

This book is dedicated to every brave woman worldwide who uses her story to glorify God and share the love, hope, and power of Jesus Christ.

My prayer is that this book will pull your heart closer to His; that you will be encouraged, inspired, and empowered to share your story.

What would happen if we were vulnerable enough to tell our stories?

What would happen if we were brave enough to break free from the pain and shame of our past?

What would happen if we were bold enough to let Jesus heal us, redeem even the darkest parts of our lives, and give others hope that He will do the same for them?

Your story is the key that will unlock others into their healing, freedom, and deliverance.

Don't hide it.

It's time for you to tell your story.

Foreword

Janice has done it again! This devotional is filled with the presence of Jesus as freedom spills from each page. Janice has created a platform for women to **TELL** the world about the power of Jesus. I have had the honor of traveling and ministering with Janice. Her heart is truly for women. She leads by example, running alongside them as she cheers them on their journey. This devotional is filled with the goodness of God and the transforming reality of vulnerability. Maybe you are in a tough season battling guilt and shame from your past. The Bible tells us we are overcome by the blood of the Lamb and the word of our testimonies. Let these courageous women's stories inspire you. I promise that you are not too broken to be wrapped up in the healing power of Jesus. Your story matters; you matter, and I am so proud of Janice for creating a space for women to break generational curses, run past the world's pains, and into the Kingdom. This space of "talking about it" brings renewal and offers a beautiful gift of freedom through Christ. If you picked up this devotional, welcome. Your life is about to be changed for the better. I pray that your story will bubble up and you will gain the courage to share it with someone else. You are not alone, friend, hand in hand, let's TELL the world about our Jesus.

—Anna Pranger
Founder of Stirred Up Ministries, Author, and Podcast Host

Table of Contents

What is a life apart from God?

Lost. Dark. Void.

For so long, I was resentful toward Christians because I went without hearing the truth of the Gospel, without someone sharing the Good News of Jesus with me. Now I use that experience to make sure that I'm the believer who takes every opportunity I can to share Jesus with those in front of me - whether that's a telemarketer, a homeless person, a hotel clerk, or a mom at the grocery store. So many have yet to hear the Good News, and I want to be sure no one escapes my presence without encountering His.

I didn't get saved until I was 29 years old in what I call a "Carny to Christ conversion." I was a carny, traveling the country with my husband, Al, and living my life aimlessly. My husband was the epitome of a nomad, and by default, I was, too. Life wasn't all bad. I have so many rich experiences, like visiting many national parks (Al's bucket list) and making ends meet by whatever means necessary.

At the height of my darkest seasons, I began attending a metaphysical school and became involved in transcendental meditation, yoga, and other occult and new-age practices. Through that, I became demon-possessed.

But God.

He always planned to rescue me from the clutches of darkness and convey me into His marvelous light!

In Natchez, Mississippi, I encountered the one who had pursued me my entire life, even when I was utterly unaware of His love, grace, mercy, and power. I was encouraged to read the book of John, and God used the power of His Word to save my soul. I was radically born-again, delivered from demonic possession, and became a fiery, charismatic believer and lover of Jesus Christ.

God is faithful and wants to save and deliver you from darkness, too.

CINDY ECKHARDT

Cindy Eckhardt is a fiery, passionate lover of Jesus. She highly esteems God's Holy Word and is a woman of passion, zeal, and tenacity. She believes God's resurrection power is active today and that He wants the body of Christ to fervently covet the gifts of the Holy Spirit, letting them always be on display in our midst.

Cindy is the founder of One Step Ministries. She ran a successful youth outreach for over ten years and several community outreaches to the poor, addicted, and homeless. She leads Bible studies, loves animals, and loves to travel.

I had lost everything.

It felt like my life had been ripped out of my hand instantly.

I was broken down, battered, bruised, and depression settled in.

What was this life like? I came from divorced parents. I saw more relationships fail mainly because I never saw a proper one. And now, I found myself coming out of an abusive relationship, and all my self-worth was depleted.

I was just a shell of a person.

I sat back and looked at my life. How on earth did I get here? Where was the woman that I used to be? The woman who was full of life, dreams, goals, and talent. My baby's life was on my shoulders, and it felt too much to bear. I had this beautiful life I created looking to me for hope and strength to be the one to provide and nourish him, but I was shattered to pieces.

Then someone told me the void I was missing was the joy of the Lord.

So, I began searching for Him, not knowing what I would find. All of my life, every man I encountered had failed me somehow, but I knew I needed someone to free me, to rescue me from myself. I began to pray and read my Bible. That became my livelihood. All I wanted to do was be in His presence. I was happy and became a better mom, sister, and friend with Jesus by my side.

Then one day, it happened. God freed me from my darkness. He gave me so much joy, light, and happiness. I can't fully explain that moment and its greatness, but time stood still, and truly the joy of the Lord was upon me. It was amazing, spectacular, and the most life-changing thing I've ever experienced. If I had doubts about God being real, they were demolished at that moment.

I will forever be grateful that God left the ninety-nine to find the one, and, at that moment, I was the one He found.

CHANDA KRAFT

Chanda is a fiery woman of God whose passion is to see others burning brightly for Jesus and living their lives sold out and surrendered to Him.

She is a mom to three beautiful children and a wife to Adam. She loves music and has a heart for worship. She loves to travel, eat delicious food and spend time with her friends and family.

Follow Chanda @chandakraft.

My life shattered on February 12, 2019, when my ex-husband head-butted me and broke my nose.

Brokenness was a gift that happened to me. It caused me to seek a saving grace.

It caused me to let go of the idea and plan I thought I had for my life.

It caused me to trust God wholeheartedly and lean not on my understanding but His.

Before the shattering, I was a bitter, resentful, angry, hateful woman in a toxic marriage where we verbally and emotionally abused each other. I lacked vision and purpose, wallowing in self-pity and self-hatred. God rescued me by taking what was meant for my harm and destroying and using it for my good.

He is still weaving pieces together into His masterpiece. He gave me life, passion, and vision for the life He has planned for me. He became the lover of my soul, restored my faith, and gave me the strength to love and forgive myself and others.

He has healed me from my hardened heart and broken life. He has taken my mess and turned it into a message of healing, hope, abundant grace, and joy in the journey.

I was a shell of a person, and He transformed me into a joyful, inspiring, impactful woman!

CINDY HOLBROOK

My name is Cindy, and I am a joyful, inspiring, impactful woman. I am a butterfly. What that means to me is continual transformation, growth, and beauty in my strengths and weaknesses. I am a powerful woman. My superpower is being a single mom of 3 amazing people. They are a driving force to keep allowing God to mold me into the mother and woman He has designed me to be. My vision for my life is to help single mothers, support them in finding their faith, their vision, and their passion for life, and help them heal and develop healthy relationships. I am also a fitness fanatic. I compete in bodybuilding competitions in figure and physique classes. I love the structure and community of athletes in the sport. My relationship with God is the only thing that has given me purpose, healing, and restoration.

It was a beautiful fall evening while riding my motorcycle when an oncoming car ran a light and crashed into me. As a result of the near-death accident, life as I knew it ceased to exist.

I grew up a simple girl who loved adventure. My parents taught my siblings and me to work hard, serve and respect others, and love Jesus. When I was first introduced to Jesus, I didn't understand why He would die for a wretch like myself. I was scared to death of God and had no idea who Holy Spirit was.

For decades, I did the best I knew, mostly checking all the boxes regarding church and having a relationship with Jesus. All that has changed since the night of the accident. As my body lay mangled in the middle of a busy intersection, I experienced a supernatural encounter with God, Jesus, and Holy Spirit. It was beyond miraculous and something I'll never forget!

That night was also the start of a multiple-year journey of physical recovery. I should never have survived the accident where both legs were severely mangled - one leg barely hanging on. The trauma to my body was excruciating, and the years of prescription drugs wreaked havoc on my brain. It was a vicious cycle of never-ending turmoil. It took nearly four years before I could walk again without assistance.

I failed to mention that a year post-accident, I got a deadly staph infection and lost my lower left leg. A month later, I lost my marriage to divorce, lost my home, and lost my ability to work. My recovery consisted of physical, mental, emotional, relational, and spiritual trauma.

Little by little, step by step, I began to apply all I learned from the spiritual journey, the night of the accident, with the process of physical recovery to all areas of my life. I can't begin to explain how God has worked in and through my life. I'm forever a work in progress - thank You, Jesus!

God didn't cause the accident, but He's used it to transform my heart. I wouldn't trade all that I lost; my marriage, my home, a limb, etc. for the miraculous journey I've been on.

I would gladly exchange Barbie doll legs or a bazillion dollars for the spiritual encounter I had the night of the accident and the journey since.

I'm humbly honored that God chose me to tell His story through mine. I pray it touches hearts, changes lives, and saves souls. Whatever your battle, it's not the end; in Jesus, there is victory. The first step, surrender, is always the hardest. Are you willing to step out in faith and see how God will transform you and use your life?

It's truly miraculous!

SHEILA PRESTON FITZGERALD

Sheila Preston Fitzgerald, author, speaker, and tragedy coach, shines the Light of Life. Whether she's encouraging one-on-one or speaking to an arena full, Sheila's gifted ability to bring her incredible story of healing into another's journey inspires everyone with unforgettable hope.

Audible, Print, Ebook of "One Foot in Heaven": Finding Hope in the Hopeless available on Amazon.com.

My gift: The first two chapters of "One Foot In Heaven" FREE at www.OneFootInHeavenOnline.com

My childhood was spent attending church every Wednesday night and twice every Sunday. We didn't have much money, but we were loved and cared for.

I attended a Christian school from elementary to high school and was diagnosed with a learning disability during those years. I was borderline ADHD and was a visual learner. A lot of what people said to me I didn't hear because my brain was always going too fast, so trying to take tests or study was challenging for me. I had special homework because of all this, which made me feel very inadequate and, to be real, just plain stupid.

I had such low self-esteem because of this, and I wanted attention from people and did whatever I could to get it, including lying and stealing. When I turned 16, I started working with a bunch of kids from a public school in the area and started receiving the wrong kind of attention from boys. One boy (who had already been sexual with 11 girls before he met me) paid extra attention to me.

One night I snuck out to see him and ended up having my first kiss and the first time all in one night. I desired him to like me so badly that I gave him everything he wanted. After that, I became sexually active and started loving that attention even more. My idea that sex was how someone showed they liked you became a sick mindset of mine that, to this day, has been a challenge to overcome.

The boy I began this relationship with was killed in a car accident just after his 18th birthday. This completely wrecked me emotionally. Giving yourself to a boy at such a young age was bad enough, but losing him after just a year was even worse. I was too young to understand any of these emotions, so I began diving even deeper into trying to get attention from men.

By 17, I became pregnant and was utterly terrified of what my parents would say or do, mainly because I was in a Christian school. Out of that fear, I decided to go in front of a judge and ask to be permitted to have an abortion (I was under 18, so it was either go to a judge or ask my parents).

I was 4 months along when I had this horrific abortion. It left me scarred so deeply because I could see the whole thing happen, and after realizing it was a developed baby, I was destroyed.

I became a woman who did not care about anything anymore. If I could be that monster, what else do I have to live for? By age 18, I worked as an adult entertainer (AKA stripper) in many clubs across the United States. I would travel all over to work in these horrible places. By age 20, I had two more abortions because of pregnancies by men I didn't even know. I did not care about my life or anyone else's.

My friends at the time were all part of the "rave" crowd, so they were using drugs like ecstasy, cocaine, and heroin. I started using ecstasy and selling it during that time. By the end of my year as a 20-year-old, I was a full-blown cocaine addict, along with every other drug I could get my hands on.

For the next 7 years, I became a prostitute who knew nothing but getting up every day and trying to find money to get the needed drugs. I lived in many hotels while selling myself to hundreds of men. Every month I would end up in the hospital with some infection or disease. I am 5'6 and only weigh 92 pounds.

At 27, I became pregnant for the 5th time (one miscarriage, three abortions). I didn't have money for an abortion, so I kept the baby while using the whole 9 months of the pregnancy. I had never forgotten when my baby was moving all around, jumping back and forth inside me from all the drugs I was ingesting. Suddenly, something (God) sobered me up, and I began to pray for her.

It was 5 months after I had my daughter, and my family found out how badly I was on drugs. They placed me in a Western Michigan Adult/Teen Challenge rehab, where I spent 14 months learning and memorizing the Scriptures. When I walked through the doors that first day, I felt like I was walking into the arms of Jesus.

I finally felt free!

After leaving the program, I was in Bible studies and had a great full-time job for 7 years. I love God with everything in me! In 2008, I married another previous addict who began using right after we got married and overdosed 5 times during our 4-year marriage. The 5th overdose took his life. After the horror of all that, I again fell back into drugs and wanted to die so badly.

My addiction was 100 times worse in that year and seven months than it had ever been. I was choked and raped during the times I was staying in a crack house. But even again, God reached down and rescued me from my mess using a stranger. To this day, it amazes me how it all happened. The stranger who helped me never laid a hand on me and helped me get back to my family and the Western Michigan Adult/Teen Challenge.

I was depressed to return, but God brought me through and took my depression away. He gave back the joy the world had stolen and made me know my true worth.

I didn't need the attention from men; all I needed was my Heavenly Father to be in my life and to trust Him with every situation that came my way. I ended up working in the ministry that introduced me to Jesus for 3 years, and I still love helping other addicts when they need it. I have been going to high schools and talking to students about making good choices at a young age and telling them all the consequences you have of making bad ones.

I am so grateful to be alive today, and I know God is why I am still here. He saved me because no one else could. I saw so many miracles during 12 years of addiction that would take 100 more pages to write down.

God never left me, and I know that He never will! My daughter is now 18 years old and perfectly healthy! I have been sober for five years and don't plan to return!

REBECCA SLAZEK

My name is Rebecca Slazek. I am 45 years old and from Grand Rapids, Michigan. I was born and raised in an Assemblies of God Pentecostal family!

I recently married the love of my life, Ron!

Connect with Rebecca via email @rebecca77morris@gmail.com

"In Him was life, and that life was the light of all mankind. The light shines in the darkness, and the darkness has not overcome it." —John 1:4-5 NIV

Have you ever struggled with something so great, real, and profound that you began believing it was your life's strongest source? Even if you wanted to be free, no other thing was strong enough to pull you out of it and grant you freedom.

Maybe it's lust. Maybe it's depression. It might even be doubt or fear. For me, it was anger. I had become entangled in deeply rooted anger and was riddled with bitterness and lies! I hated who I was when I became lost in an angry rage. It felt as though I had no choice or control when disappointment, low self-esteem, and feelings of being misunderstood would build up in me until an eruption of anger took place. I could only stand by, wait while it ran its course, and then deal with the aftermath of my rage.

I had known the Lord most of my life, raised in a Christian household, believing in Jesus and wanting His love. It was not until I fully surrendered to Christ in my teens that His beautiful Spirit revealed the lies I had believed for so long. Lies that sounded more like truth my whole childhood! The Word of Truth (through the Bible) began to wash me and reveal the truth to me. I took on the mind of Christ and began to see more clearly that my anger was only a deception of strength and that God was stronger than all things! Everything laid under His authority! He was replacing my old ways of doing and thinking with new ones! It was then that I could see that a great source was available to me!

It was JOY!

How could something so sweet and innocent be stronger than anger?! God showed me that it was part of His nature-it was embedded into the fibers of who He was! And if it was part of the very nature of God, then He could give me access to as much as He'd like! Joy is a fruit produced in us by the Spirit of God (*Read Galatians 5 for my details*), and being part of God's nature, it has more authority and power than anything found on the earth!

Even my anger!

I finally saw the truth. The Lord's Joy is my strength; I received it to the fullest! This truth ran off the darkness that had tormented my soul for so long. Anger left me, and with it went bitterness and lies!

I saw myself for who I was in God's eyes and could finally walk in the truth of who He said I was a child of God, set free from sin and the entanglement that it brought me! When I begin to feel overwhelmed by anything...and I mean anything... I can turn to the Truth, Jesus, and HE, in return, will overwhelm the very thing that is overwhelming me!

Darkness has fled from me, and I am filled with the light of Christ!

He is my JOY!

"To Him who is able to keep you from stumbling and to present you before His glorious presence without fault and with great joy." —Jude 1:24 NIV

JESSICA PAYNE

Jessica Payne is from southwest Michigan, where she and her husband, Matt, reside with their three children and their dog (Todo) and cat (Stormy). Jessica is a worship leader and has written original songs, including one she sang to Matt on their wedding day. They have been youth pastors for many years and are very involved in their community.

Jessica loves the beach, quality time with family and friends, and talking. She is incredibly gifted at counseling women and loving people like Jesus. Jessica has a beautiful gift of hospitality; if you know her, you love her.

I thought I'd never be free.

For ten years, I struggled with bulimia — and, before that, years of disordered eating. The first time I threw up, I was 22. I knew it was wrong, but the lies in my head said otherwise.

Is it that bad? I got rid of SO MANY calories! How can it hurt if I only do it once in a while?

So, I did it again. And again.

At first, I thought I had control. Purging felt empowering to "make up for" occasional binges. But, occasionally turned into daily. Sometimes multiple times per day. All I could think about was my next binge. That was my comfort zone. My high. Till purging sucked the life out of me. Such a vicious cycle. It consumed me like an addiction.

I knew I'd lost control at some point, but I still believed the lies.

This makes me happy. I don't want to stop.

My relationships suffered. I withdrew from family, friends, my now ex-husband, and God. Praying, church, worship... all made me feel like a hypocrite. The Holy Spirit's conviction weighed heavy on my soul every time I gave in to bulimia. I knew it was idolatry. But I did it anyway.

Maybe six years in, I reached a turning point. Physically, mentally, spiritually...I was exhausted and trapped in a life that felt like death because I wasn't living. When I imagined my future, all I saw was bulimia.

In hopeless desperation, I pleaded with God to take it away and make it stop because recovery seemed too impossible. I didn't trust Him enough to get me through it.

It took a few failed attempts to recover before I finally broke down.

God, I can't live like this. I know I have to trust You with my fears, insecurities, cravings, all of it. So, I'm letting go and trusting Your way.

God's way led me to a book that offered hope through someone else's recovery story.

I stopped bingeing and purging one day a week, then two, and so on, till I went an entire week. Then a month — and I never went back to bulimia after that first month of freedom. I clung to God while allowing myself to sit with the emotions and withdrawals and not give in. He was my strength in weakness. I hoped that freedom was possible. I repeated His truths in my mind till they replaced the lies.

Now, fully recovered, I know God never left; I left Him. So many times during my ten-year battle with bulimia, God put situations in my path to steer me toward recovery. But every time, I rejected — and even resented! — His help.

Yet, God is a patient, loving, gracious Father. He embraced me like a prodigal comes home and saved my life... a second time. Today, I TELL the world of His grace and victory because He entrusted me with this story.

JAYME MULLER

Home is Knoxville, Tennessee, where I've fully embraced my inner mountain girl (after growing up in Michigan and living in Florida for five years).

In 2020, I met my now husband, John, who also loves to travel, hike, and embrace the adventure of everyday life. Together, we travel quite a bit and also own a motorcycle.

So this is me, a Tennessee girl (+ her guy and our dog) with a passion for everyday and far-away adventures—and trusting God through it all.

Follow Jayme @adventureandthegirl & @hopeandthegirl and visit her website at adventureandthegirl.com.

I had known Jesus most of my life. But I met Jesus at thirty-five years old.

Being raised in a home where religion ruled, fear reigned, and abuse was a way of life, this was the foundation of my belief system. These generational shadows and pain echoed the choices and situations I would find myself in, deceived and searching for answers. Watching the death of a loved one, my heart wrestled with what was on the other side of the grave. I started to seek truth, and there, I met Holy Spirit and a tangible Jesus, a heavenly Father.

Page after page, verse after verse, the Bible started to come alive to me in a way I had never experienced. It led me to get still and wait for His presence, words, and truth.

Through hardships and divorce, empty promises, and loss of hope, I struggled to get free from the reality of my circumstances and did not know how to connect what I read to be true in the Bible and the fight it was to keep a smile, provide for my children, and keep breathing.

Jesus waited.

For me.

Over ten years ago, after this loved one passed, I became hungry for more of Jesus and the truths from the Bible. For several nights I would put my kids to bed, go into my office and place a chair in the center of the room.

I dimmed the lights and prayed, "Lord, I know you're up there. Would You show me what this Holy Spirit is?"

And then I sat in silence. And listened.

After a few nights, Jesus met me there. He had been waiting for my heart, for me to seek Him first. Before work, before pastors, before books, before anything.

That encounter marked me for life.

His presence was so tangibly real. It was the first time I felt an unexplainable love I had never known before.

Seventeen months ago, I was sitting in a hospital bed during one of my life's most challenging seasons. Diagnosed with an unexpected spinal cord tumor, a seven-hour surgery, a long recovery, and now new normal shattered what I believed would be for my future. The question I repeatedly heard in my heart was, "Do I believe what I believe?" I wrestled with fear and anger, unbelief and sadness. I know I will not have the answers for the why or what the suffering was for, this side of Heaven.

But Jesus understood. He took it. His grace covered it all.

In those hard times and loneliness, Jesus will hold it all in His hands, patiently waiting for us to look into His eyes and believe again.

In times of devastation, whether disease or divorce, diagnosis or brokenness, this is where the mystery of the deep things of Jesus and His Word reveals the truth. The greatest way to combat life throws at you is to get along with Jesus. Throw out the checklist of religion and fix your eyes on Jesus. Be still and truly know that He is everything you need.

Jesus is waiting for you. All of you. All of the mess, all of the pain, all of the lies, all of everything.

Ask Him.

He holds your heart.

APRIL DAWN

April Dawn desires to lead women to the Bible to hear from Jesus. Her heart of simplicity takes root in Indiana with her husband, three children, and gardening. She obtained a B.A. as a Minister of Christian Counseling through journaling with Jesus at Christian Leadership University.

She has published three books: Never Forsaken, Listening For Jesus In Your World

Listening For Jesus In A Teen's World

You can follow her blog at: everydaythreadsofseedsgritandgrace.com

"The soothing tongue is a tree of life, but a perverse tongue crushes the spirit." —*Proverbs 15:4*

Words can hinder us. It starts with a negative thought that enters our mind, and if we do not take it captive immediately, we then start to believe it as truth. This negative thought can come from our thoughts, what others have said, or Satan himself. The enemy loves to use our own words to destroy us by believing his lies as truth.

I struggled greatly in this area when I first accepted Christ 22 years ago. I would tear myself down with the power of my own words. I would constantly complain, murmur, grumble and speak negatively. I knew I needed freedom. I knew my words mattered, but I didn't know how to change my words.

God led me to Romans 12:2, *"Do not conform any longer to the pattern of this world, but be transformed by the renewing of your mind."* I didn't grow up in a Christian home, and communication was amiss. The only words used were critical or negative, so the pattern of negativity became a deep trench in my mind.

My transformation was slow, but God helped me with every step. God began to show me that my words have power (Proverbs 18:21). We need to choose to speak life daily; over ourselves, our struggles, and those around us. To speak life, I had to retrain my brain with truth by breaking all the lies I believed about myself, God, and others. The only way to renew my mind was by obeying God's Word.

So, instead of rehearsing the lie in my mind, I would pause and ask myself, "Is the thought I'm having a lie, or is it the truth?" Sometimes I didn't have the answer to this question, but I would choose not to rely on my feelings to lead me, but instead go to the Word of God to get clarity.

By knowing, believing, and acting on His truth, we are set free (John 8:31). It's not enough to only know the Word of God; we must also believe what He says is true and then act on it. We act on it by speaking His Word out loud to break the negative pattern in our minds. This is a daily choice; this is not for the faint at heart. But this is for those women of God who are warriors, ready to take a stand, and who say, "I'm not letting the enemy wreak havoc any longer in my mind. I choose to speak life!"

If you struggle with your words, know that you are not alone; we all struggle! Give yourself some grace, but don't stay there. Take action and let God teach you how to turn it around. Freedom and joy are waiting for you on the other side of this mountain, my sweet friend. I encourage you to rise and speak life! Speak God's Word over yourself, your struggles, your job/finances, your marriage, your children, your relationships, your body, your past, present, and your future!

I chose to step out in obedience, out of my comfort zone, and speak life out loud, and a breakthrough came! I was set free, no longer crippled by my own words or those spoken over me. I found freedom and joy! John 8:36 says, *"He who the Son set free is free indeed."*

JENNIFER ELSTON

Jennifer has been married to the love of her life, Jason, for 21 years and is the mother of three teenage daughters. She enjoys family walks, game nights, crafts, and reading good books.

She has been a credential holder with the Assemblies of God since 2000. Currently, Jennifer enjoys traveling to speak at local churches and women's conferences while serving alongside her husband Jason as Children's Pastor at Holland First Assembly in Holland, MI.

Jennifer has a huge heart for seeing women become equipped in their giftings, find rest in Him, and thrive as Godly women in their homes and local churches.

The Word Saved My Marriage.

My marriage was not a very good one. When I first got married, it was for all the wrong reasons. A week after my marriage, my husband wanted a divorce because he was still in love with his previous wife. I was devastated, but at the same time, I did not want another divorce. I had been married before, so I decided to stay in the marriage and fight. Had it not been for this marriage, I would not have returned to the Lord nor learned how to pray or study the Scriptures, so I am grateful to a certain extent for what I went through.

One day, I heard a woman of God speak on Christian television. She explained how you pray the Scriptures, which caught my attention and gave me hope. I started accumulating them when I read the Bible and made my promise book. God showed me there was no magic in how many times I prayed the same Scriptures, but what happened was faith was being developed in me. At first, my husband came to the Lord but was hurt at church and backslid, making it even worse. I just kept going with God. I felt drawn to Bible college, and God opened a door for it to be paid for while my husband kept drifting further away.

Some days I just wanted to quit believing in him and my marriage. One day I was walking out of a store and said, "God, I am done. I can't do this anymore." He asked me if I would stay for Tim's soul, and I said I would.

After Bible college, I was sent out to start a church with the support of my mom, dad, and close friends. Tim still did not come back to God or the church. Eventually, he started returning and now leads worship and is beside me in ministry.

The seven years I went through before he returned to God were difficult. He did things many women would have left over, but I chose to stay. I realize not everyone could have done what I did, but God gave me the grace to endure. Now I encourage women to stay in their marriages if possible and stand on the promises of God until they come to pass.

One day I spoke to the Lord and said, "I am not going to ask for anything today, God; just give me what you think I need." A day later, I woke up to my husband sitting on the couch crying. He said, "you know we did not get married for the right reason. I did not even love you then, but I love you now. Will you marry me?"

Well, the rest is history. He planned a whole wedding to renew our vows. He arranged doves, a guitarist, a singer, a bed and breakfast, and so on.

I guess God knew what I needed.

LORIE NICHOLS

Lorie Nichols is the Apostle/Prophet of House of Refuge Church and the founder of Lorie Nichols Ministries. She is married to Tim Nichols and has two children and 5 grandchildren. She is passionate about ministering the Word of the Lord for encouragement, healing, and breakthrough. She enjoys spending time with family and friends. She and Tim reside on their small hobby farm in Hillsdale, Michigan.

Find more information about Lorie's ministry at www.hhorc.com.

I would describe my testimony as the Bible verse, "My brethren, count it all joy when you fall into various trials, knowing that the testing of your faith produces perseverance. But let perseverance have its perfect work that you may be perfect and complete, lacking nothing." —James 1:2-4

After graduating high school, I accepted the opportunity to move to Hamilton, AL, to attend Ramp School of Ministry (RSM). While I was thrilled about what God would do in my life that season, I was unaware of the process I was about to endure.

I was raised in a unique and loving family. Yet, like all families, trial and tribulation came knocking at our door. Around my senior year of high school, I began to see a decrease in my dad's faith in God. When I left for RSM, I was worried. The lack of faith in my dad had begun to take a toll on my parent's marriage. For months of RSM, I spent it face down on the floor, crying to God to turn my father's heart from stone to flesh again. To make him sensitive to the Holy Spirit so that God could move in his heart again. Yet, it seemed like the more I prayed, the worse the situation would become. I was discouraged. This pain and intercession continued during both years of RSM until I moved home after graduating.

I came back to Kentucky in May 2019. My family was still falling apart. I was anxious about coming home from a spiritually healthy environment to chaos like it was. Yet, I took what I learned in school and implemented it. I learned my authority over the enemy and his stronghold over my family's lives and began tearing it down for good.

I began to pray harder. I remember James 1:2-4 because it promised me that I would see God's promise that *"as for my house, we will serve the Lord."* Prayer after prayer, the tension would get strong, but God gave me a vision of myself holding a rubber band. The more tension I put on it, the closer it was to its breakthrough.

So I went to war with the Devil.

Then in January 2020, my dad had an encounter. He came home from service, and God moved upon him. He was broken, he apologized for his carelessness, and we forgave him. From that moment on, I saw God answer every prayer I prayed for 2 and a half years before my eyes. My parent's marriage was restored. We began to go to church together as a family again. We could step behind my dad as the leader of the house and trust he was listening to the voice of God. And most of all, I saw God being glorified.

I'm forever grateful that we can cling to God's promises. Even when trials are hard and we want to give up. Through the testing of my faith, perseverance was produced, and I watched my faith being put into action and bringing my dad home to The Father, the almighty God.

He can and WILL do it for you also. If you believe in a miracle in your family, don't give up! That prayer could be the one that puts enough tension on the rubber band to snap it and press forth your breakthrough.

Claim it.

Receive it.

He will do as He has promised you.

AUTUMN TRICKLER

Hi, my name is Autumn Trickler. I have lived most of my life in Berea, KY, but I moved to Hamilton, AL, for a season to attend The Ramp School of Ministry from 2017-2019. I recently married my husband, Adam Trickler, in October of 2021. I am also a dog mom to a good boy named Kash Money.

Philippians 1

Roe vs. Wade overturned. I rejoice, and I am thankful that my mom chose my life. People who I love and have served are not rejoicing with me. They believe "a woman's body is a woman's body," and they have sought through social media to educate me on why abortion is important. I read a heartbreaking story about a mom carrying a baby with painful seizures in her womb and how she scheduled an abortion so her baby would not have to feel the pain. After the overturn of Roe vs. Wade, her doctor called and canceled the abortion. One of my former students wrote a quick message before forwarding this attachment, asking why the "Ass Hats" would do this, and the article shared why abortion is necessary.

This post touched my heart deeply as I was expecting a baby in April of 2005 and sadly birthed him unexpectedly on December 7, 2004. Had he lived, he would have had many serious situations to overcome-sight, hearing, and physical strength. No matter what, I loved him and trusted God to provide exactly what he needed. He was born perfect for his age development, and my husband and I held him tight until his heart stopped because no lifesaving procedure would keep him alive. It was all in God's hands. It was a sad time. No one wants to lose a child, and my husband and I were about to have our 12th anniversary, so having a child was special. It was so comforting to have the time we had with our baby, to hold him tight, kiss him, love him and speak wonderful, loving words to and over him. I shared my story from a place of vulnerability as I responded to the post. I shared that I understood this situation and was so thankful I had the opportunity to hold my baby, and I will be forever grateful.

I responded, "I am happy for you, but..." I replied, "don't be happy-it was the saddest experience for me. Grief was hard, but I am thankful to have that time with my baby to grieve and heal. I shared my story to help the mom who shared her challenges because I thought it could help." Immediately, he shared condolence and prayer hands, and my reply to him was with grace, "I believe we are both trying to help people in our way."

I have a purpose, and you do too. My husband and I lost a baby, and somehow the sadness of that loss has always shown Jesus amid grief, health, and the opportunity to have the son we have now. God can use any situation to shine Jesus and the Gospel through you. God loves you beyond measure whether you are pro-life, pro-choice, the woman on the fence, the woman who is unable to have children, the woman who is excitingly having a child with a family telling her it is irresponsible, the woman who found out the child could cost her; her life and chose to abort, the woman whose world has been turned upside down with her child's heart stopped beating in her womb, the woman who is looking at a positive pregnancy test and has an abusive partner, the woman whose abortion haunts her every day, the woman who was raped and is pregnant with a child...to ALL the women, God loves you beyond measure.

He wants you to seek Him and His wisdom because there is grace, knowledge, and love in Him. He wants us to choose life and see how He will shine in each situation. He will give you the fruit of the spirit - love, joy, peace, patience, kindness, goodness, temperance, and self-control. No matter what, He loves you beyond measure. Philippians speak to a time when some will preach Christ from envy and rivalry, but we are to do it in love. As you read social media posts, don't waiver. Know that you were created with a purpose, so love others, and you will know and discern the truth.

JOSIE SMITH

Josie Smith is a Professional School Counselor of over 20 years. She has been married to her husband, Chip, for 30 years and their son Hunter attends Kellogg Community College.

Josie loves Jesus, working out at the gym, and visiting with friends. She is thankful for coworkers who start the school week praying for students, staff, a hedge of protection, grace, and the Holy Spirit to work in and through them.

DAUGHTER

I started going to church when I was 15. At the time, I wasn't sure what compelled me; it wasn't even a conscious thought, just something I started doing. I was curious about this God I had always heard about on television and in movies but didn't know personally. I would always stay over at my friend's house so I could go with her family on Sunday.

After some time, I ended up at the church God would later root me in. I recall this one time when I was 16 or 17; I was at the altar when a woman I had not spoken with came up to me to tell me the story of the woman with the issue of blood. How this nameless woman was the only woman or girl in the Bible that God called daughter, and she heard Him call me daughter. This is one thing I carried with me when I was disconnected from the Lord. "The first time God spoke to me, He called me daughter."

I believe He was planting this seed of love and hope that I did not understand at the time because of my limited knowledge and understanding of who God was. He was preparing me for where He knew I was about to walk. The loveless, broken, abandoned places I was going to take myself. I was going to walk through a valley of despair and hopelessness. But what my spirit knew that my mind didn't comprehend was that I would always have a place in my Father's House.

There is this one instance that comes to mind. I was a young mom in a relationship I should have left behind long ago. A situation happened that I don't recall the details of, but I remember getting in my car and driving to the church. I don't remember making the conscious choice to drive there; I just left my house, and the next thing I know, I'm walking into the church. Regardless of my physical mind, my spirit always knew there was safety in the House of the Lord.

As we see in Isaiah 30:18-19, God was waiting on me so He could move in my life. I didn't know much, but I knew I could not commit to God until I upheld my commitment to Him. So I would go to church for long periods until I returned. But I always knew I would be welcomed. I always knew I had a place to go. My Heavenly Father has always known me and the heart He gave me, and He planted the seed that I would never understand until I built an intimate relationship with Him. That all along, my Father loved me and looked out for me. My Father was waiting with open arms for His beloved daughter to come running home.

ASHLEY AUSTIN

Ashley Austin is a mom who loves to travel, read and learn new things.

Ashley is integral to E4N's School of Ministry, helping with administration. She also supports many ministries within her church and is a part of a dance ministry.

More than anything, she loves Jesus!

My name is Melissa. I had parents who loved me, plus two older sisters who tried fiercely to protect me. As a young child, I was fragile. All I wanted was love and acceptance. However, I was met with bullying and rejection. I had no confidence in who I was. My parents had serious health issues at home, so I drifted into the shadows, accompanied by pain and despair. I drowned my bed in tears, rocking myself to sleep. I found comfort at times by drawing, reading, and writing. These things still couldn't silence the nagging thoughts that this world would be better off without me...and that I would be better, too.

I was so emotionally unstable and isolated. It got worse when I found out my mother died at age 17. Losing her broke my spirit. She was my everything. This took me on a path of hopelessness and darkness. My pain blinded me to the evils around me. I was desperate to escape this new reality of life without her. I was then abused by a man who did and said what he wanted. It was with him that I discovered alcohol. I found my escape. For a moment, I didn't have to remember the trauma. The loss of my mother was heavy and the abuse added to the torment. It was confusion and chaos.

I faced sexual trauma resulting in a pregnancy. I was addicted, mentally ill, and just utterly broken. From program to program, I would go looking for something to fix me and looking for hope.

There have been flickers of light throughout my life, even amidst the trauma. All that I had been looking for, I found in Jesus. It is grace that met me where I was. My journey took me to a faith-based program called Amanda's House in Three Rivers, Michigan. I was surrounded by genuine love and acceptance. Here the Lord opened my heart to expose the depths of my painful roots. Then my healing journey brought me to the doors of SPA Women's Ministry Homes in Elkhart, Indiana, where I have truly surrendered my entire being to Jesus. No longer do I live defeated but victorious! God has revealed who I am through wise counsel, mentoring, Bible studies, and much more. I am His! He is mine!

My wounds testify to God's redeeming love and redemption. I am not a victim of my circumstance, but I am an overcomer!

Today, I am a working woman shining bright for Jesus. Steps are being made toward financial peace. Restoration of relationships is taking place. Difficulties are faced with faith and hope. No longer do I want to die. I am a new creation living boldly for the cause of Christ!

And when I look in the mirror, I don't see a mistake...I see a woman with a beautiful heart, longing to help others get free!

"You have turned my mourning into dancing...I will give thanks unto you forever" —Psalm 30:11-12

MELISSA PARKER

I was born in Wayne, Michigan, to my mom and dad, and I have two older sisters. Yes, I'm the baby! I lived in Romulus, Michigan but grew up in Belleville, Michigan.

Since a little girl to now, I have loved animals...cats are my favorite, with dogs in second place. I love cute furry animals! I love to draw, read, and write. Always have. Although now I love reading and writing about Jesus. I love learning about God.

I still have a thing for stuffed animals. Yes, I can admit that.

I love to walk. I can walk forever and ever. It's time I can spend with God and look at the beauty of his creation. I enjoy spending time with the people I love. I especially love being in church and worshipping God together.

I love to encourage, inspire, and help God's people. I want nothing more than to be a light and share Jesus. I want to spread love and hope.

When I was first asked to share a piece of my testimony for this book, I thought of many things I could share. It isn't easy to pick just one portion of my testimony because, in my opinion, my testimony is still being written. Each day another piece is added, and the growth is continual, but I will try.

I grew up in a Christian home, although my parents were trying to figure it out too. They did not choose to follow the Lord until they were married and parents. They had a lot to learn, just like most of us. My mother later told me that my insistence would often push them to go to church.

My mother was abused when she was little and had repressed the memories, so as she started to remember, it was very hard on all of us, and she needed a lot of help. While this was happening, our church was also experiencing some issues. I had gone to that church most of my life, so my parents' decision for us to leave was hard.

I started dating a young man within this church. He proposed fairly quickly, and we married the following February. I was only 18 when we got married.

Before we married, we had gotten in a car accident, and my fiancé had been severely injured. He ended up with a closed head injury and severe burns. Because of this, he stayed home, and I was the one who was working.

One day, I came home from work, and he was upset about something. In one violent move of his arm, he threw everything on top of the dresser onto the floor. At that moment, I knew I was in trouble.

After that, the physical abuse started. I won't go into all the details, but I know there were times when God protected me even more than I realized. I never knew when the next incident would happen, and that alone brought fear. I would pray to God at night to just let me die.

I stayed until some time right before my 21st birthday.

One day, he called my dad and told him to come to get me - a total and complete miracle. You would think this would end my troubles, but it just worsened. Being in such a broken state, I did not make good decisions. I started smoking and drinking and became very free with my body. I tried for five years to hide all the pain I had, all the while rejecting God while He whispered my name.

I was not going to do *anything* someone else told me to do.

I continued to heap more pain onto my already broken self. We can be abused by someone else, but if we don't allow God to heal us, we can also abuse ourselves.

This is where God and I met when I realized that my life, trying to run from Him and anyone else who would tell me what to do, was making things so much worse.

So, I finally turned back to God, and He began to heal me.

He can heal every part of us. He does such a great job that most of the time, we don't look like the broken mess we were. He will even heal the wounds that we create ourselves.

It hit me hard just recently, when I was thinking about writing this piece, that even when God heals us, we still have to forgive ourselves.

So, I encourage you today to let God forgive you and choose to forgive yourself! God wants to give you joy for your mourning and beauty for your ashes. (Isaiah 61:3)

BONNIE BELSON

I have been married for 21 years to my amazing husband, Kevin. I have two boys who are complete miracles and nine years apart! I prayed for both, but I had to pray a lot longer for the second one!

I love to share my testimony with women. If I am vulnerable and tell what I have been through, they can see what God can do for them!

If God can make my ashes beautiful, He can do it for you too!

I learned to see myself through my stepdad's eyes, and my worth was weighted by shame. I carried it like the woman at the well. She held the weight of the clay jar on her shoulders, empty yet heavy with brokenness. I carried my shame in the bottomless pit of my jar, waiting to be filled at the well with living water.

The shame balanced on our hips just as we endured the heat to avoid others' opinions because we are so good at tearing each other down as women. We throw shade in the moment of heat when God is calling us into unity.

The clay jar represents the emptiness we carry daily to the well, only to be emptied and filled as a dysfunctional cycle. The well was more than that! It represented the power of purification! It quenched the soul; it aligned the deep, dry roots that puncture the heart.

We come parched, spiritually dehydrated, broken, and weary. We walk strategically toward the beating sun as our feet are dirty, kicking the dust off this old dirt road, branded and alone.

And then I saw Him.

There He was.

My mom was in denial and wrote me off to teachers, counselors, and family members as a liar and unstable. Like the woman at the well, we go through things for so long that people call us by our circumstances, not our names. Jesus meets us at the well to free us from society, family, and friends that shackle us to our circumstances.

He was in the sun's gaze, waiting for the Samaritan woman, for you and me! To liberate us and empower us, exhort and deliver us. When Jesus gets us alone, there are no naysayers.

It's just you and Him.

He meets you at the well, in your secret place, in the prayer room, at the altar, in your circumstances. It's never just rainbows and flowers-He's a God In the middle of your storm, with the needle in your arm, when the blade breaks the skin, intoxicated, high, in the middle of your gossiping. He's waiting at the well to call you home and your daughter.

Will you meet Him at the well?

ROSEMARY RUIZ

My name is Rosamaria Ruiz. I have the privilege of raising two children in a Godly home and came to know Christ myself at the age of 9. I enjoy being around family, whether it's immediate family or church family. I love to fellowship.

I have been in ministry for 6 years and serve in various areas, from Youth Ministry, Dance Ministry, and Intercessory Prayer, as well as volunteering time with Ephesians 4 Network to contribute to the next generation of youth.

The last few years have been a doozy. I have never felt so beat down, exhausted, broken, hopeless, and unworthy. First of all, I was raised in a unique Christian home. My parents are incredible followers of Jesus, who loved and taught my siblings and me so well. Many believers and non-believers that I have spent much time with have assumed that because they knew how I had grown up, I would not struggle in the same ways as someone who had a challenging childhood would.

This caused me to set an incredibly high expectation on myself to "perform" the way everyone expected of me, always attempting to reach for perfection outwardly and spiritually. Despite my efforts, the battle began with knowing what God wanted for my life, genuinely wanting the same for myself, and fighting the temptations of worldly desires. When I failed to follow through on my commitments to my parents and God, I would fall apart mentally, emotionally, and physically. I had such a strong desire to walk in God's footsteps and the plans He had for me, but I would find myself trying to collect myself off the ground again, striving to get back to what God had for me.

This became my pattern. I have now had multiple sexual partners; I am recently divorced and pregnant with another man's baby. It is so crazy that I am even writing about this to you. Only six months ago, I probably would have said no, feeling entirely unworthy of showing you how God has radically revealed Himself in my life. I would have said my testimony is "**broken**." You would have found me sobbing on the bathroom floor, yelling at myself, and criticizing myself for my actions because I KNOW BETTER. I have been given everything I ever needed to walk a "perfect" life in Christ, yet I am battling immense anxiety, trying to hang myself on my cross. It is hard to share a lifetime's worth of hurt and struggle amidst a relationship with Christ in only a few paragraphs, but it is not all doom and gloom.

This life is hard, and the enemy is so real. Yet, at the end of it, all God has repeatedly shown me is why HE was the one to bear our cross because we literally can't. He asks us to come to Him as we are, all the brokenness and sin.

The crazy part is He doesn't leave us broken! We never intended to experience the hurt this world brings, yet God can turn our brokenness into beauty. He has and is doing that in my life, and He can do it in yours too.

Even before He made the world, God loved us and **chose** us in Christ to be **holy and without fault in His eyes.** God adopted us into His family by bringing us to Himself through Jesus Christ. He wanted to do this, and it gave Him great pleasure. (Ephesians 1:4-5)

AUDREY MEAD

My name is Audrey Mead; I am 23 years old and have grown up in Michigan my whole life. I am so excited to share a piece of my story with you. I am super outgoing, my family crosses me into the little bit weird category, but I embrace it! I am so in love with my Jesus, although my walk with Him has been far from perfect. But I love how He has allowed me to become the bubbly and crazy person I am today, using my experiences to grow and shape who I continue to become.

As I sat, I could see the doctor's mouth moving. I could not hear his words, but I knew exactly what he was saying as he confirmed what I knew to be facts. This wasn't the first conversation, doctor's visit, or even the first time the word "cancer" had been thought of. I knew the first time I felt a bump in the side of my groin precisely what it was. In the pit of my stomach, I knew. I prayed it wasn't, but I couldn't shake the feeling.

That evening I stood in the bathroom staring at my reflection. I could see the bulges in my neck. One had grown into three. I could not deny it. They were there, staring me in the face. I remember thinking a thousand thoughts all at once. Hearing them in my head but not being able to give words to them. I had no voice. I did not understand. How was I gonna tell my kids, my husband, my mom? It had all happened so fast. Symptoms started in December, and I was getting tests, scans, and biopsies by February. Confirmation of a diagnosis came in early March. I felt like Job. Really? This? Now? I had had enough. My daughter had had severe health issues for at least the past 2 years. I was torn between "why me" and "why not me? Am I no better than anyone else"? And then it happened out of nowhere. I cried loudly, "I DO NOT WANT THIS, TAKE THIS FROM ME." It was despair, desperation; brokenness that I had never felt before was coming out of my mouth and bouncing back at me.

After what seemed like hours of crying, I felt at peace. It was a peace I didn't quite understand. I remembered the Scripture; I remembered the garden. Is this how He felt? Knowing the Father could deliver, heal, help, and rescue, but would He? Did I even deserve the right to ask for help? Had I brought this all on myself? Was this a reflection of me, my sin, my brokenness? I thought of the crucifixion. Jesus had gone through way worse, and it wasn't a reflection of anything He had done. I was also brought to John chapter 9. Here a man was made blind not because of his sins or the sins before him. He was hand-picked to display the works of God.

Through his story, Jesus would shine the light of truth, the light of hope (I now feel this could be the case for me. I hope it is).

I believed our Father was loving and the giver of all perfect things. This didn't seem perfect. Scripture kept flooding my mind before I even realized it. Romans 8:28 is one of my favorite verses: "and we *know that all things work together for good for those that love Him.*" I loved Him; I knew that. I prayed and asked to be healed. I asked that, if at all possible, my children, and my family, be spared of the hurt and pain that this could cause. I was 38 years old with 4 children. This would be 4 children without a mother, a husband without a wife, and a mother without a daughter. The thought was more than I could bear.

This time it was Jeremiah 29:11-14, *"for I know the plans I have for you...plans to prosper you and not to harm you, plans to give you a hope and a future. Then you will call upon me and come and pray to me, and I will listen to you. You will seek me, and you will find me when you seek me with all of your heart. I will be found by you."* When I prayed, I prayed harder, not for me but for my children and my husband. I started to pray and accept whatever the plan may be. I prayed that it be done according to the will of the Father for the good of my family. Not knowing what that may be, I focused on praying for my children's future mother. She would be kind and loving, and she would love Jesus and raise my babies to love Him. I was certain only I could that she would love my husband in a way. I prayed for joy. I needed to be able to choose joy even on the hardest of days.

Fast forward about 18 months, and I still have some bad days. I have learned that my specific cancer is something that I will probably die with and not from. There is a battle that is consistently fought. With every little bump, fear sets in. It's hard not to examine lymph nodes daily. I more than likely will have recurrences and bouts of remissions and relapses. I am still going through treatment that makes me tired and ill. It has affected my memory, my relationships, and my body. I still pray that I will be healed with all aspects restored one day. Until then, I have learned not to ask "why"; instead, I ask "what for?" How will this be used? Who can this help? Standing on John chapter 9, it won't be in vain.

I do not believe this is for nothing. It will be used for good, and I hope to find out sooner rather than later what that good is. Until then, a few verses that I am standing on would be Isaiah 41:10, Psalm 73:23, and

Psalm 32:7. In Hebrews chapter 12, we get a glimpse of what being steadfast looks like. Jesus never loses sight in this chapter of where He was headed so He could put up with anything along the way. This is how I stand, how I keep going. It doesn't matter what I face here. I will not lose sight; I will keep going. I invite you to stand with me and pray.

Heavenly Father, we come to You and ask You for Your comfort, touch, and favor. We ask that You help us not to lose sight. That You help us to focus on You and Your will. We ask that Your will be done in our lives and those around us. We ask that You use us in whatever way is needed to further Your Kingdom. Even though we do not know Your plan, You do. We may not be able to see it, but You have orchestrated it perfectly. We trust You; we love You. We believe You have our best interest at heart and submit to Your authority for whatever that may be. Please help us not to demand to know the whys but to ask to be shown the what for. Lord, reveal Your purpose to us. Give us joy amid our pain and sicknesses; Lord helps us choose Joy. You are our Joy. We love You. In Jesus' name, amen.

AMANDA BEACH

You can find Amanda in a small town at the base of the mountains just southwest of Salt Lake City, Utah, where she and her husband are raising four wonderfully amazing children. She works for a multi-site non-denominational church, South Mountain Community Church. This is where you will find her demonstrating her love for people while serving as the Support Services Director and the current Women's Ministry Leader. Amanda likes to travel, read, sing, and love babies in her free time!

I was born a timid girl. I would follow girls around because I wanted friends, but they would always say, *"Can't you talk?"* and *"what's wrong with you?"* But God has been pulling that shell off me. I not only talk one on one but even to whole groups of people now. I have freedom because I have no spirit of fear, but power, love, and a sound mind.

Recently, I walked down the street in Detroit, Michigan, and went up to two girls. I said, "Jesus loves you, and I love you. I bind and break every word curse that was spoken over you. I release the anointing and the fire over you, now." Then I said, "Do you know Jesus?" I quoted John 3:16- *"For God so loved the world that He gave His only begotten Son, that whoever believes in Him shall not perish, but have everlasting life."* Then I told them to say this after me, *"Jesus forgive me, come into my heart and life and be my Lord and Savior, in Jesus' Name."* One girl said it and then looked at me, saying, *"Do you know I'm addicted to crack cocaine?"* I said, *"Do you want to be free from it?"* She said, *"yes."* I commanded in Jesus' Name for the spirit of addiction to go, now! She said, "Do you know where the garbage is?" She picked up this box and ran to throw her drugs away as fast as she could.

One of the first times I went out of my comfort zone speaking to people was at Applebee's with Cullen, my evangelist friend. I would follow, praying for him and learning, but this day when I saw him talking to the owner, I knew we were about to be kicked out soon. Cullen still had two more tables with about 12-15 people to pray for, so I thought I'd better pray, or we might not get to them. After I finished, I walked up to Cullen, who told the owner we would leave after he prayed for the two tables. I told him I already did. His jaw dropped. He couldn't believe it and was so proud of me. I was pretty happy, which pushed me to pray for bigger crowds. The harvest is ripe, but the laborers are few.

I never thought I'd be out on the streets (especially in Detroit), but God has turned my life around. I'm a single mom who was away from God. Three years ago, the stress of my bills piling up made me rush to the E.R. because I couldn't breathe. The doctor said it was anxiety. So then I knew who it was! The Devil comes to kill, steal, and destroy. God gives LIFE! So I found a church. They prayed over me, and I felt that spirit of fear that had gripped my life come up and out of me. Jesus set me free! And you can be, too. God is no respecter of persons. Just give Him your whole heart.

STEPHANIE RITTER

Hi, my name is Stephanie Ritter.

I am 43 years old. I am a single mom to three girls, Emily, Genevieve, and Mattie. I have six brothers and one sister. I wouldn't say I like demons, and I love seeing people set free.

When asked to give one's story, I have to ask people to narrow it down. I believe that people's lives consist of chapters, and depending on where you are, some chapters can make up a big part of your life. But for me, most pages are either blank or only consist of a few sentences. My battle with depression, anxiety, and PTSD started at a very young age, and the extended undiagnosed symptoms developed into considerable gaps in my memory. Some of what I remember, whether good or bad, inspires me to be who I am today. So where does the life of the given come in? I knew I was set aside for the Lord from an early age. More often than not, you would catch me alone by myself—most of the time, that was all I had; myself and God. I spent so many years in isolation that I became socially awkward. I would start random conversations with people in odd ways that just made people uncomfortable. Because of that, I spent most of my life getting bullied in school, beginning in elementary school and not tapering off until my sophomore year in high school. Over and over again, I would try to fit in but could never quite understand why I wasn't accepted. I was always told my opinion didn't matter or that no one wanted to hear what I had to say. I started believing that I didn't matter. So I began to pour myself out into music and studying God's Word, but the depression still didn't lift.

Throughout it all, one thing was constant. I could hear the voice of God, and I knew He wanted me to be His own and to keep Jesus as my Lord and Savior. Throughout my walk with Him, the ups and down, and every obstacle, He has always been that constant. I'm so happy He called me into ministry at an early age despite my struggles, insecurities, and fear of speaking in front of anyone (which would cause extreme fear). He still desired to use me. I'm so happy I answered the call to go forth.

My journey in ministry has, in many ways, been a trial by fire. I first started preaching inside an all-male maximum security prison. This made me love God all the more. I remember getting a lot of pushback from people telling me that "those people" were locked up for a reason. "They got what they deserved" or "Everyone has a jailhouse religion until they get out" were just a few phrases I've heard over the years.

I realized from that that it wasn't just the inmates locked up in prison but those who said they were free but were honestly spiritually bound. God would use me to minister within male and female prisons, juvenile detention centers, children's homes, drug and alcohol rehabilitation centers, and places where there were victims of human sex trafficking for years to come. But not how most people would think. Creative Arts. That is where I gained more confidence in the Lord, but I didn't know that I also started using it as an opportunity to hide.

You see, my encounters with people were few, and amid ministry, few knew I was still struggling with depression, anxiety, and PTSD. I learned early on that in the church; it's simply something that stayed hidden because someone that broken surely couldn't be used by God, right? The Lord showed me that it was OK to be who I was for Him, and He would heal me in due season. Not that I was being punished but that I was being used as a testimony for others. Once I realized that, I felt like a heavy weight had been lifted. Now, for over 14 years, I've been preaching the Gospel and ministering in song, both in and out of the United States. It hasn't always been easy, but it's been worth it. I learned it's OK to give all of me for Him.

That, my friend, seems like such an uneven trade, but in God's eyes, I'm worth it.

DANYELLE SPEAKS

For this woman of God, music and preaching have grown to exist in perfect harmony. Danyelle began in music as a teenager and released her first Jazz CD at age 16. By age 21, she had her first record deal but was disappointed. This style of music was pulling her away from where God was leading her, which was preaching and music that uplifts the Kingdom. After losing the record deal, she began seeking God for direction and finally accepted her calling as a preacher. Danyelle was ordained in 2010 as a Minister and decided, instead of seeking another record deal, she would continue her pursuit in the industry as an Indie Artist. Since then, she has released 3 C.D.s with great reviews and continues to travel, preaching and singing the Word of God.

In 2019, to pursue another passion, she became the co-owner of a production company named Brown Sugar In Your Coffee LLC, where she is the videographer and editor. Now she produces music videos, interviews, and podcasts for various clients.

> *"Sometimes the smallest things take up the most room in your heart."* ~ *Winnie the Pooh*

There was a period in my childhood when my mother was a single mom. She did whatever she could to care for my two siblings and me. It was a struggle. I remember one night, we were in the middle of a terrible snowstorm. There came the point when we ran out of gas on the side of the expressway. My sister was just an infant then, and Mom knew there was a good chance we would all freeze if we stayed on the side of the road. She felt it safer for us kids to stay in the locked car while she went for gas. After she gathered her little money, she began a 5-mile trek to the gas station and back.

It couldn't have been more than 10 feet into her journey when a set of barely visible taillights pulled up to her. This car was full of hymn-singing, Jesus-praising church ladies. They bought us snacks, let us get warm in their car, and refused to let Mom pay for the gas she poured into our car. Looking back on it now, those wonderful ladies gave me my first glimpse of God.

Years later, we lived in a run-down trailer park. I remember there was this blue bus that would go around and pick up kids on Sunday mornings. From time to time, my siblings and I got to take this bus and ride to the local church in town. I had no idea who Jesus was, much less had any relationship with Him, but much like the church ladies on the side of the road, I knew there was something special about these people. They were filled with such joy would still be more than a decade before I truly understood the joy I had witnessed and from Whom that joy had originated.

Moving into my adult years, my little family and I regularly attended my boyfriend's church. Praise the Lord for his mom's patience, and fervent prayer landed us there.

It should be noted, though, sitting in the pews on a Sunday morning doesn't make you a Christian any more than sitting in a garage makes you a car. See, while those prayers managed to get me in church on Sunday, she couldn't pray me into a relationship with Christ. That was a choice I had to make on my own.

Not long after that, I found myself in the middle of a breakup from my relationship. The church I had been attending was my boyfriend's; I thought this was my only connection to God. I was so lost and broken, and I didn't believe He wanted to talk to me anyway.

One day, I was coming out of Kroger when a smiling face stopped me. I recognized the pew in front of me on Sunday mornings. I expected she would be angry with me, but instead, she let me know I could sit with her and that their church was my church too. There was no judgment, no looking down her nose, just God's love and grace. It still brings tears to my eyes.

She, like the others, had no idea that her simple gesture of love and grace would profoundly impact my life. This woman, those ladies on the side of the road, the bus driver, and all those people at the church all made such simple acts of kindness, but their priceless gestures were a beacon of hope to this girl who didn't know Jesus.

Today, I am confident that these moments paved the way to our reconciliation and eventual marriage, the growth of our family, and, most importantly, my salvation. I pray that throughout my life, I can pay forward the generosity of that group of church ladies in the car or that I could be a bus for someone so they might have a path to knowing Christ. I also pray that God will help me do those things with the grace and love of that beautiful smiling lady from the next pew. When our simple gestures reflect God's grace, the truth of His love shines brightly.

NIKKI PALASZESKI

Nikki Palaszeski has been in children's ministry for nearly a decade and has recently broadened into women's ministry, including event planning, hosting online women's studies, and speaking engagements.

Nikki Palaszeski is the wife of a pastor currently serving Union City and Athens United Methodist Churches and a homeschooled mother of two girls.

I was born in Kansas to a ministry family. Growing up, my parents were the youth pastors, and my dad was our church's worship leader. So, it was pretty natural for me to be in ministry. Some "ministry kids" grow up and walk away from God. I had my moments, but I always felt the pullback. For me, things got rough around 9th grade. In a short period, so much had happened. We were a family of 7 when my mom was pregnant. We had a house fire; my brother was born shortly after the fire and soon passed away, and my dad cheated on my mom. They ended up getting a divorce, leaving me to feel like my world was crumbling around me.

From here, we moved to a completely different church than the one I grew up in. I was immediately asked to start serving in the church. At around the age of 15, I was placed as a leader in the youth group and over helping with any dances of the church. When I graduated at 17, I decided to come to Midland, MI, for Bible schooling to continue in ministry. Although I graduated at 18, I was asked to stay as a youth leader. I would chime in and out (depending on where I was in life).

I found myself in a "Godly Relationship" where I was head over heels in love. We had been together for almost two years and planned to get married. Because we were long-distance (him being in Michigan and me in Kentucky) for most of our relationship, we could commit to staying abstinent. But towards the end of the relationship, I was asked to give in. I didn't want to lose him, so I gave in.

I remember being so frustrated with myself. So upset with us for letting this take place when we had made a decision and stuck to it for so long. In the end, I felt worthless. He said he never really loved me and used me solely for my body. After speaking with leaders, he explained that I could never be someone that would "fit" into his family and that of leaders. And because I was a young black woman, it would "just never work."

I was devastated!

I went into a horrible depression.

I eventually went to college. When I got to college, it was a year and a half after all my friends from high school had already started college. I was living about 2 hours from home on my own for the first time. I ended up clinging to the only person I knew, a young man I had only seen in passing in high school. We would spend A LOT of time together and eventually end up in a relationship. Things escalated so fast. I knew I wasn't ready for a relationship, but I felt alone. In all our time spent, I could trust him. Unfortunately, things went south even faster. I was choosing to live abstinent (again), and he was tired of waiting. This ended horribly with him raping me. I blamed myself the first time and tried to forgive him. It continued on multiple occasions. This made me very angry. Angry with men, angry with myself, and somehow, angry with God.

I decided to leave him and college—too many OBVIOUS bad memories for me. I found myself back in my tiny town and desperate for a change. My mom constantly encouraged me to go to church. I returned and confessed all I had dealt with and was battling to my youth pastor. She encouraged me to continue being honest in my walk, seeking counsel, and trusting God (although it may get complicated). So, I did.

As time went on, I found myself even more in ministry! I was asked to be an official youth leader and was given the youth worship team to lead. The closer I found myself drawn to God, the more I began to find my purpose. God had my heart, and that's all that mattered to me. Watching the teens grow in Christ showed me I was on the right path.

Along the way, I was so blessed to meet my husband. It was spoken over my life that I was going to meet my husband. At the time, I was placed in charge of a band for our church's annual Purity Conference. I was told that by trusting God all this time, who He had intended for me was coming. The following year, my husband ended up coming to do a show at my church (he's a DJ for his friend, a Christian Artist). We met, got engaged, and married in a year (which I DO NOT recommend, but I am truly grateful for all I've learned along the way. HAHA).

Almost five years later, I am happily married, have my two-year-old son and a baby girl on the way, and serve as a family in ministry. Nobody HAS TO go through hitting rock bottom to find God. Unfortunately, I did from the choices I made. But in the end, God had me. He chose me. I just had to choose Him. My worth doesn't come from those around me and the Father who created me.

ALYSON EVANS

My name is Alyson Evans. I have been leading worship for a little over ten years. I currently serve at the Edge Urban Fellowship in Grand Rapids, MI. Before that, I served at Abundant Life Church in the SUPER small town of Radcliff, Ky. I grew up in the church. My parents were youth pastors, and my dad was the worship pastor. As I got older and found my voice, I moved into leading worship and being a youth pastor. I was over the youth worship team at Abundant Life and assisted in training the teens to use their gifts for the glory of God. Now I am a wife and a mom of two. I am a full-time worshiper and a Doula. I love helping others! I travel and help lead worship at conferences and churches; I love every second of it!

I'm FREE! I'm FREE!!

What Jesus did for me:

As a girl born and raised (until the age of 12) in a Catholic home, I knew of Jesus. I knew of a seemingly faraway being who was supposed to love me so much He died for me. Why? So I could go to heaven instead of being condemned to hell.

Because of this sacrifice, I learned I should go to mass every Sunday for 45 minutes. I should sit, stand, and kneel when prompted, sign the cross, take communion, and sing the hymns without falling asleep on my Mom's shoulder as I sat idly on the pew. I should mind my manners, repent of my sins (to a priest), pray to the Saints and Mary for my spiritual needs, and bake a dozen cookies for the old folks home once or twice a year so I could earn my annual forgiveness. I didn't have to change how I acted daily; I just had to fulfill my weekly checklist, and I was as good as a citizen of Heaven for eternity!

I didn't realize until many years later that I wasn't being taught about Jesus. I was being trained in tradition. I was taught about manmade rules of how to access God.

'Do this; get this.'

Religion.

After many years of searching, the Lord led me to persons, situation after situation. Little by little, I came to the life-changing realization that God is not dead, Jesus is accessible, and the Holy Spirit is still in operation today! I didn't need to pray to Saints, or Mary, for God to hear me. I didn't need to tell a priest the few bad things I would disclose to him on the annual day of repentance. I could talk DIRECTLY to Jesus!

My mind was blown as the revelation of this knowledge cascaded like a waterfall through my dry, barren spirit. Me? Can I talk to God? Can he talk back to me? Why hadn't anyone told me this before?!

My life has NEVER been the same since, and each day gets richer and richer as He faithfully guides me from glory to glory.

If you take away anything from this short testimony, let it be this:

Don't let ANYONE tell you that the Holy Spirit is no longer in operation today.

Don't let ANYONE tell you that you can't speak directly to Jesus or that God doesn't hear you when you pray.

Read your Bible. Let it be the only ruler with which you measure truth.

I spent several precious years of my life learning about religion instead of the relationship God had designed for me all along. My life completely transformed when the truth of the FULL Gospel found me. I say, 'found me because God has been pursuing us since before we took our first breath.

There is hope. There is freedom. There is always MORE! Whatever you're facing today, the Lord is your solution. *'He works ALL things together for good for those who love God and are called according to His purpose.'* (Hint: That's YOU!) - Romans 8:28

BROOKE GRESKOWIAK

Well, hello there! I'm Brooke! Pleasure to meet you! So, who am I, you ask? Great question! It may have taken me a minute to get here, but the Lord is showing me how to love being 'me.' It feels great! He's shown me that I don't have to assume the false identity the world thinks I should have and has shown me how to embrace the glorious way He made ME. I don't have to wait until I'm the right weight or have the right level of education, income, or job title before I can be used effectively for the Kingdom and enjoy my life!

My life is simple. I'm a girl from Northern Michigan who loves Jesus, my husband Andy, my family, my dog (Chaos), the great outdoors, dad jokes, delicious food, laughing, fall leaves, bonfires, and exploring new places! I love seeing people make decisions for Jesus and boldly walk out their faith in everyday life! I love seeing how God, time and time again, leaves the 99 for the one. I've been that 'one,' have you? I've seen the Lord work in mighty ways in my lifetime, but more than ever in the last year! God is undoubtedly on the move, and He's working things out for your good every day! He sets the captives free; He loves beyond comprehension. He's the Prince of Peace. He's our shelter, our firm foundation! I could go on and on...but you get the idea. I'm so happy you're here! You're worth it; you're loved
from the beginning.

My names is Nakato Kasine Sheilah. I have a twin sister, and I'm from a humble, ideal polygamous family. I am the firstborn to my father and second from my mother out of 16 siblings, ten dads, and six moms. I was born and raised in Kampala, Uganda, in East Africa. I grew up in a small neighborhood.

It is every child's dream and wishes to grow up in a family with two loving parents to care for them and to look up to, but unfortunately, that wasn't the way it was for my siblings and me.

My parents met when they were still in high school. Life was hard for them, and it wasn't long before they separated ways and had to look for other partners. They both remarried, and we were separated from our mother amidst the confusion. At the tender age of two, we were taken to an orphanage when mom didn't know how to care for us. It was hard for her. She prayed a lot and believed in God, and after five years, she got to see us again.

Mom was married to another man, and because of that, our grandmother took us to her home in a Kampala suburb. She taught us morals, prayer, and manners, which I am grateful for. Every discipline I have is because of her. She was a committed, born-again Christian who would take us to church every Sunday.

Many traumatic memories and hard times motivated me and pushed me to improve. Amidst all the turmoil and torture my siblings and I faced, I could still attend school. The fights between my parents gave me trauma, and at some point, I lost concentration in class for two terms and faced depression and frustration. I didn't realize until I became an adult that it caused so much pain, hatred, and low self-esteem. As a young woman, I finished high school by God's grace.

Growing up, I had a dream of pursuing law at a university. I always thought it might happen someday, but my stepmother told my father that there was no money for school for us older children since her young kids were also in school. So it took me another year to figure out what to do If I didn't join a university. Meanwhile, I applied for scholarships as I also believed in God for a miracle, which happened! Isaiah 55:8-10- for His ways are not our ways.

God connected me to the lady to who I preached. Later, I got to teach her how to pray, and she received JESUS as her personal Savior. She asked me what I do, and I told her about my life. She was touched and paid for my tuition at university for the first year! I was excited and happy! There was a time when I had to stop attending for a while, but I eventually got a tuition-only scholarship. At times, my father would send me money to help with food. I eventually graduated with a bachelor's degree and a second upper degree. Isn't God amazing?

My work as a humanitarian has impacted me to love and help the needy where I am able, all because of JESUS. He has enabled me to do a project that looks after vulnerable people, single mothers, and children abused in the southern part of Rwanda. This has helped me to grow spiritually, learning to love those who feel unloved, not to get something out of them or for what they can do in return. It's all about the compassion, kindness, and love we share as Jesus did for us. I love to do God's work.

With all the turmoils of life and challenges I faced growing up, Jesus saved me from resentment, bitterness, rage in my heart, depression, sadness, and emptiness. I have changed my whole outlook on life because of JESUS. The feeling that I was never loved had low self-esteem and was ugly, and all the surrounding negativity left me, and I have become more positive. Above all, I have learned to forgive by God's grace and prayer and by the power of the Holy Spirit. He led me to a prayerful life, revealing the power of the cross that still amazes me.

KASINE SHEILAH

Kasine is from Rwanda, Africa. She loves listening to music, especially country and gospel. She loves cooking and trying new cuisines and recipes. Her passions are traveling, long road trips with loud music, and good friends. She enjoys meeting new people, praying, and is a hugger.

Sacrifice wasn't a word I heard a lot growing up. It wasn't the center topic at our dinner table or part of our car rides to school. I have learned that walking with Jesus comes with many sacrifices, and I mean a lot, and to be honest, no one ever told me that I would have to die to myself. I don't remember my parents telling me, "Kristina because Jesus laid his life down, you're going to have to lay yours down too!" If you were a little kid hearing that, you would be scared out of your mind. Say again?

I have to leave and lay down the life I think is best for me and lay it down as a sacrifice but pick up a new life in Jesus. Growing up, I don't think I ever heard the words life and sacrifice in the same sentence, and I wonder why that is. Why isn't the word sacrifice discussed much regarding our walk with Christ? Why would anyone lie without a biblical foundation to back the reasoning?

The definition of sacrifice is the word "zebah" in Hebrew, meaning slaughter (the flesh of an animal) or an offering sacrifice properly. The word has different sacrifices; sacrifice of righteousness, strife, dead things, covenant sacrifice, etc. It is important to look up the definition of words to understand the context and, for an even deeper study, study the Bible in Hebrew (Old Testament) and Greek and Aramaic (New Testament). The Google definition of sacrifice (the noun) is the "act of slaughtering an animal or person or surrendering a possession as an offering to God or a divine or supernatural figure." But the verb definition is "offer or kill as a religious sacrifice."

So it's a verb; when something is sacrificed, it's an action taking place, and because Jesus was the ultimate sacrifice, he offered his body. Romans 12:1 tells us that "Therefore, I urge you, brothers and sisters, given God's mercy, to offer your bodies as a living sacrifice, holy and pleasing to God—this is your true and proper worship." We must sacrifice our bodies to God because we are now alive in Christ. Our old spirit is gone, and now we are new, and that is why we are living sacrifices because of the light in me.

I saw God move powerfully, and He answered this prayer I was waiting for and forgetting about. But, I wonder why God answered a prayer last week when He could have easily done it any other time before last week or when I prayed it that day. Because, in this case, a sacrifice was made between him and me. I had to lay down something in my heart that I knew He told me to let go for a minute (new destination He is calling me to go, and I wanted to go to this conference) and focus on a specific area of my life; my family.

"*Obedience is better than sacrifice,*" and it truly was at that moment. Looking up that verse, 1 Samuel 15:22, the proceeding verse is a little scary. 1 Samuel 15:23 says, "*For rebellion is like the sin of divination, and arrogance like the evil of idolatry. Because you have rejected the word of the Lord, he has rejected you as king.*" The Lord was rejecting Saul as King, by the way. Rebellion is like the sin of divination (witchcraft) and idolatry. I don't want to have any trace of rebellion because after disobedience comes rebellion.

But, because I had obeyed sacrificially in what I felt my spirit was led to do, God answered my prayer two days into focusing prayer. Man, I broke out into praise like no other while driving, and tears were rolling down my face (not safe!), but I couldn't wait until I got home to praise the Lord for this answered prayer! Isaiah 62:24 says, "*Before they call, I will answer; while they are still speaking, I will hear.*" He hears you, and God hears you in the smallest of prayers. Say this with me; *God hears me.* 'Before they call'- so, before you even ask, God knows that you're going to ask it, already has the answer, and is ready when He wants to release it in His divine power. I can never forget that moment. Amazingly, God answers and hears us, so don't stop praying.

God is so faithful and if you're waiting on an answered prayer, wait on Him. It is a sacrifice of your desires to wait on God, but let me tell you, the answered prayer came unexpectedly when I wasn't thinking about it, paying attention to it, wasn't asking God about it (and it is so funny that I don't like surprises, so God knows me well). So, the fact that He surprised me with this answered prayer shows that He truly knows me more than anyone in the world, and He is so awesome as our Abba Father.

KRISTINA RENEE

Kristina is a fun and energetic teacher who encourages women to flourish in their purpose. The most recent author of "Strength In Him" from her daily quiet times with The Lord. Kristina wrote this to encourage women to know where their strength comes from. Her educational background started her love for teaching God's Word and her desire to travel the world speaking his Word. She is the founder and CEO of Spiritual Healing Sisterhood, Inc. Their mission is to see women healed, restored, and set free. Through mentoring and discipling in a small group setting, the sisterhood has the heart to see women grow, be empowered, and be healed from past hurts and trauma.

Kristina is also the founder and CEO of Learning Styles Academy, whose mission is to serve students with their God-given gifts and learning styles. She is passionate about seeing students learn, grow, and have fun! Kristina is a seminary student at Dallas Theological Seminary and hopes to use her degree to impact women's ministry and Christian education. Kristina lives by Psalm 37:23, "The Lord makes firm the steps of the one who delights in him," because she knows God is the only one who can make her steps firm.

Follow Kristina and her journey at www.kristinareneexo.com and on Instagram @kristinareneexo.

I restlessly open the drawer to a credenza in my bedroom. I stare at the random contents and shut it as quickly as I jerked it open.

I don't want to deal with that right now.

Noticing the irony, I sigh deeply, exhaling another layer of defeat. Like my marriage, I prefer to leave that drawer shut and ignore the random crap there for another day, month, or year. Not because I'm emotionally lazy or in denial. I'm quite the opposite: As a therapist, I pride myself on being emotionally fervent and kind-of-sort-of in complete awareness. It's just too much sometimes.

After 28 years of turmoil, strife, resistance, prayer, and tears (with some good times and laughter sprinkled throughout), we've discovered that my husband is on the autism spectrum. His brain is wired differently than what's called "neurotypical" humans. He doesn't connect with others; he constantly masks to fit in with co-workers and family members—to appear "normal"— and then is exhausted at the end of the day from said masking, thus creating the perfect emotional petri dish for breeding hatred, frustration, impatience, intolerance of change, and no energy for investing in a relationship.

This discovery happened about three weeks ago from the time I wrote this. In those weeks, I have felt relieved, confused, enlightened, compassionate, and grief-stricken. I've developed a new perspective, connected with a support group, delved deep into disappointment, examined my co-dependency, and begun understanding my husband in a way that helps me not take things personally.

I've also been angry, depressed, hopeless, and anxious. I'm trying to embrace my situation and work towards being hopeful, joyful, and free, but this grieving process is downright daunting.

I realize that what I've been hoping for all these years—an intimate connection with my spouse—isn't going to happen. I thought when we make better money...maybe when the kids grow up...when the kids move out...when the grandkids get older... when he retires...maybe he'll see me, know me, enjoy us. But, alas, it isn't going to develop the way I had imagined, hoped, or dreamt for all these years.

And contrary to a 28-year popular belief, *it's not his fault.*

Honestly, that isn't very pleasant. It's human nature to want to find an explanation, assign blame, and wholeheartedly accuse. Like the end of a game of Clue:

Takes cards out of mangled manilla envelope and holds them up triumphantly

"Ahem...The guilty party was the selfish Mr. James, who used the No-Connection weapon in the kitchen (and living room and bedroom and garage, and any given social situation)."

It's how we've been taught to find closure and move on. The only problem with that technique is that explanation without blame leaves a giant: *Now, What in your life.*

This is where, being a therapist, I get to practice what I preach and accept the situation for what it is. I'm unsure how this will end, but I must speak my truth. I mustn't hide behind the Good-Christian-Wife instruction booklet that says to be a martyr and set aside my dreams, needs, and voice to accommodate, serve, and placate. To try harder and pray more. To navigate the terrain of disappointment alone and stay quiet about the Grief that burns holes in my spirit like a California wildfire popping up again just when I thought it was put out. I am allowed to be heard, to feel, and to communicate. And in this acknowledgment, I feel worlds merging and truth bubbling up as a salve on my wounds.

Then, when I need it the most, Spirit begins the precious work of mending the holes that Grief burned. In the quiet of the night, I am reminded gently, see, I'm doing a new thing. When I'm lost in rumination, I hear He transforms us by renewing our minds (and not just neurotypical people). When my brain is whirling with what-ifs, I am reminded to be still and know.

Because the truth is this: God is my source of life and hope. My relationship with Jesus is the most intimate connection I can have. And

Spirit is always with me, guiding and healing me with wisdom and correction. I will figure out how to accept this new season. I'm sure that wherever that takes me will be the adventure of a lifetime.

JANELLE JAMES

Janelle James is an avid reader, painter, mother of two, and grandmother of six. She loves deeply and is loyal to a fault (read, recovering codependent). She is vulnerable and transparent at times but also quiet and private with others, striving always to be authentic. Being an outgoing introvert (yes, you read that right) has taught her to balance her life in a way that allows her to serve others yet be intentional about self-care. Janelle has been married for 28 years, during which she and her husband have been through a million and one awful situations and a million and two wonderful ones. They share their home with three dogs (two of which are certainly part human), two cats, and one fish. Janelle's other hobbies are golfing, writing, landscaping, and furniture rehabbing. She loves Jesus and believes in His ultimate power to change anyone's life through healing and restoring relationships with self and others. As a counselor, Janelle relies on the Holy Spirit to guide her as she walks alongside people in their pain, suffering, and healing. And she is honored to do so.

I was raised believing that my identity was defined by a man, which meant I thought I was nothing if I did not have a man in my life. When I was 18, I visited my brother in San Diego and met a man in the Navy. A few months later, I revisited him. As we drove through Las Vegas, we decided to get married. It was fun and exciting. He was a very strong Christian, and I wanted to have fun. I was not ready for the commitment. We divorced within the year.

I moved back home, used substances heavily, and found myself pregnant by a high school boyfriend. After two years, I continued to have unhealthy relationships with others. I met a man in the Air Force and fell madly in love. We also started to have a sexual relationship. I believed I was unloved by God when I had sex before marriage.

He was moving to England with the Air Force. In my mind, I couldn't lose him. We got married within three weeks of the meeting. Shortly after we moved to England, physical abuse started, and I felt stuck without friends or family. I couldn't leave because I lacked confidence in believing I was strong enough until we lived in California. A friend introduced me to another man...go figure.

This man appeared to be attentive and comforting. He was also in the Virginia Army station where I wanted to move. If we were to get married, he would be able to move all my belongings to VA, and I would have income for housing and insurance. It seemed like a no-brainer, not to mention the sex was good. Little did I know that Jesus wanted so much better for me. This man soon went AWOL, and I found myself losing everything I had worked hard for. I moved back to Michigan, the place I desperately wanted to escape from. I bounced around from relationship to relationship for a few years.

While living with my parents at 31, a man moved next door into their trailer. He was strange and always kept to himself. I did love a challenge. I found a way to talk to him. We started to have a sexual relationship. I found myself pregnant, desperately wanting to get married because it was a sin. I know, crazy thought process.

I decided he was the only one that would put up with my crap. I mean, I understand that I am pretty difficult to live with. It wasn't very good. He abused my kids physically and emotionally. At one point, we had so many open CPS cases they put us both on the registry. I knew I did not want to get divorced.

I felt like I would be a failure if I got divorced for the third time. I finally could not take it any longer. I found myself praying for help. God comforted me, telling me He has so much more for me. I felt so much peace. The process fell into place so smoothly. It was scary as he stalked me and threatened me several times. My group of women from church wrapped their arms around me.

The journey after is where I experienced the overpouring of God's never-failing love. I refused to live in the same trapped hell. I began diving into His Word, praying, and surrounding myself with spiritually confident people I aspire to be like. God has shown me that I am worth so much more. I am loved fully and completely. He has met all of my needs financially and physically. I started this journey about seven years ago. Today I find myself grateful and content with where I am in Jesus.

Even when life is hard, I know He has a much grander plan than I could ever dream. Some days, I sit back and try to imagine it. He will stop me and say, *"that isn't even close."*

I am forever grateful for His unending and unconditional love.

TRACY MCFADDEN

I have lived through rejection, abandonment, low self-esteem, divorce, and addiction until I learned how much Jesus truly loved me.

As I find myself a four-time divorcee, I have learned that my story is of the love and compassion of Jesus to share with others. I am a passionate follower of Jesus, an ultra-marathon runner, a triathlete, a mom, and a nana.

As I grew up, we went to a Baptist church. I was involved in the youth group and the Power of Love, a music/skit group that shared the Gospel message at other churches. However, I usually attended while I was drinking. I also did not understand that Jesus was truly alive.

Through my alcoholism, I was at a party with a group of Christians wanting to share the Gospel. I experienced what Jesus was about. HE IS ALIVE.

How often have you had to keep a secret? Keeping a secret can cause us to have a tremendous amount of willpower to keep a "normal" facial expression, "normal" voice, and "normal" body language, especially when the secret is something huge. There are some secrets; if other people only knew them, your life would no longer be the same. People's perceptions of you would forever be altered, so you keep the secret. It could be something you thought or did that brings shame. For the majority of my life, I was the keeper of huge life-altering secrets. In my mind, I believed that if others knew what I had done or what I did, they would reject me, talk about me, or treat me differently. So, I kept my secrets behind locked doors and threw away the keys.

Keeping my secrets changed me and how I perceived myself. I became withdrawn and hid myself and my talents to avoid drawing too much attention. If I drew too much attention, others might discover my secrets. I pushed away friends and family alike. I craved love and friendship but could not accept the love they gave so freely. I lived a huge façade all the while I was in excruciating pain on the inside wishing that others could see that pain. I wanted to stop living a life of secrets. I wanted to speak up, but fear kept me bound in the perpetual lies of the enemy and perceived rejections of family and friends.

Ever so patiently, God began to speak to me and teach me who I am. My secrets held me captive for so long because I didn't understand who I was and to whom I belonged. I was a daughter of the King, precious in His sight, created and cherished as a prized treasure, endowed with gifts that could never be taken away, and loved more than words could ever explain. I was forever changed when I understood who I was and to whom I belonged.

"Then you will be empowered to discover what every holy one experiences—the great magnitude of the astonishing love of Christ in all its dimensions. How deeply intimate and far-reaching is his love! How enduring and inclusive it is! Endless love beyond measurement that transcends our understanding—this extravagant love pours into you until you are filled to overflowing with the fullness of God! Never doubt God's mighty power to work in you and accomplish all this. He will achieve

infinitely more than your greatest request, your most unbelievable dream, and exceed your wildest imagination! He will outdo them all, for his miraculous power constantly energizes you." —Ephesians 3:18-20 (TPT)

All the reasons for keeping my secrets were shattered. The fear of revealing my secrets was replaced with a longing to speak of the atrocious things done to me to set someone else free from living a painful life of keeping secrets. God then had me take a huge step of faith to reclaim my identity and self-worth by finally finding my voice and telling others those secrets. So, I wrote my story and published it. 'Orphan No More' was me shattering the cage in which my secrets had locked me. You see, God's love had set me free, and the perceived rejection of others no longer bound me, for I was secure in God's love.

JEN KONING

Jen is the Author of the book *Orphan No More*. She has a Bachelor of Science in mathematics specializing in secondary education. Currently, she teaches middle school mathematics. Jen lives in Michigan with her three teenagers. She is passionate about helping others find freedom from their childhood trauma and sharing the Word of God with others. Jen has taught children's church for over ten years, led small groups, assisted in weekend retreats for abused women, and spoken at different events.

No one to the One!

Who I was ten years ago is not the same person I am now. There has been so much growth. All glory and honor to God! He is the One!

"He created us to do good works that He prepared in advance for us to do." —Ephesians 2:10

He saw me through all of my battles. He was with me through the neglect and the sexual, verbal, and physical abuse as a child and adult. When I was a young adult, I gave into temptations, which gave me two children and an unequal relationship that was abusive for eleven years. I drifted away from God because I felt shameful, dirty, and not good enough. I also felt alone, like I didn't have a purpose, no one believed in me, I didn't have a family, and I was this black sheep that no one loved.

But God found a way to get me back into the church, build, and show me that the church became my brothers and sisters in Christ. Then I got into another relationship and moved away with him. Then that relationship turned abusive, but this time, though, I didn't leave the church or God. This time I left him with only the things I could fit in my van and moved to a shelter that protected women and children from their abusers. Eventually, I found a home and met my husband through some friends. I believe God sent my husband to me to show me consistency and to show me a deeper understanding of what love is. Now, He uses me to share my story with others. (Psalms 139:7-10) Where can we go that He isn't? He is always there, guiding and holding us.

I am so glad I am not the one writing my story. I see now how every step, God was there giving me gifts, giving me something to uplift me and encouraging me to hold on. I didn't see it as clearly then as I do now. God sent people, and still does, to mold and shape me. But more importantly, He gave me His word to hold onto. (1 Corinthians 13:4-13, Philippians 4:6, Isaiah 41:10.) God showed me what love was, that I

95

could come to Him and He would listen, that I shouldn't fear because He is with me. Over the years, my understanding of this truth has grown to a much deeper understanding that God is so much more than that. (Proverbs 3:5). Trust in the Lord, lean on Him and His understanding. God is so much more. His word is life! The more time I spend in His Word and presence, the more I experience freedom from the battles I went through. He led me back to Him. (John 15:16, Luke 15:20.) He chose me and ran to me with open arms. He gave me a kiss, a robe, and a ring. He even changed my name (literally and spiritually). I went from victim to victor.

He did the same for you! (John 4:39-42) He knows your story. He wants to give you eternal life. He wants you to share your story so others will see Him and be saved. (1 Peter 5:7, 1 Peter 5:10). He says cast your anxiety on Him because He cares about you. Your suffering is only for a little while. He will restore you and make you strong, firm, and steadfast. Jesus Christ is the One-the One who can set you free!

"May the Lord bless you and keep you; the Lord make His face shine upon you, and be gracious to you; the Lord turn His face toward you and give you peace." —Numbers 6: 24- 26

RUTHIE PIOTROWSKI

Ruthie is a wife and a mother; family is important to her. If you know her, she will treat you like family because she is compassionate, caring, and loving to everyone around her. Life has not always been easy for her. Despite that, she has overcome and been set free because of God's love and faithfulness.

God redeemed what the enemy meant for evil for His glory and honor. Ruthie allows the Holy Spirit to use her story to speak life and ignite others around her.

Her ultimate desire is to see people set free and transformed into who Christ created them to be, to tell others they are loved, chosen, and enough!

I was born into a family where my mom was the breadwinner, and we never lacked anything we needed. Fast-forward to 2016, my elder siblings were already in the University, and everything was going fine until it was my turn to enter. After my mum's birthday, the first week of November, she stepped on poison at her business place. It wasn't a good experience because we went from an average family down to a lower-class family that could barely feed 1 square meal. My siblings were already in school, so it was just her and me.

Moving forward to January, I got a call that I had been given admission into the University. I wanted to decline the admission because there was no money and the school was quite expensive, but my mother insisted I go. So we borrowed 45k to pay for my acceptance fee. Then the next phase of suffering began. I got to the school with the money I could get from friends. I squatted with some girls for 2 years because I couldn't afford to pay rent. They were my angels in human form. They always bought me soap, cream, body spray, clothes, and so on, so I didn't feel less privileged. I would often beg for 10 naira to buy water, and some people would mock me and laugh at me.

I had no matriculation number until my final year because I couldn't pay any of the school fees, but God did it. If there's one thing I thank God for, I didn't give up or drop out. I was writing my exams and attending lectures even when I was denied access to many things in the school, including my results. In my final year, after the lockdown, my family skyrocketed back up, and I could clear all my fees from my first to my final year. I finally got my matriculation number and had to meet the lecturers so that my results could be uploaded.

Today, I am a graduate of Mass Communication from Abia State University, Nigeria. You might be going through a similar condition as mine or worse, and it's choking you, making you want to quit, but my dear, DON'T QUIT. Please don't give up because it's not over yet. It's only over if you give up. There's one phrase my spiritual father told me that kept me. He said, *"whatever you are going through isn't new. Someone has gone through it and overcame it. Surely you will overcome yours because it has only come to build you up"*.

Trust God and document it in your heart that He is too faithful to fail.

VANESSA

Vanessa is from Lagos, Nigeria. She is intentional and passionate about seeing young ladies flourish in their careers by helping them build their self-esteem and embrace their worth.

Connect with Vanessa @mma_enendu (Chidinma Enendu)

I was born in the south of Texas, where it's hot, hotter, and hottest. I am a ginger, very fair-skinned, and have blue eyes. Most people who are around me say I am a very positive and uplifting person. They say I am very happy and always try to find the positive in everything. I am someone who is all about helping others. I describe myself by saying I try not to judge anyone because you never know what someone has been through. Growing up, I was picked on because of my hair, bracing, and being a nerd.

When I was three years old, my parents divorced. I lived with my dad and my stepmom. My brother and I begged to go live with our biological mom. He finally gave in. I lived there from the ages of 6 to 9 years old. While we were living there, we were sexually abused. My stepdad and my stepbrother molested me. These "events" would happen mainly when I was asleep. I would be awakened in the middle of the night. It was quite scary to fall asleep because I feared what would happen. Imagine a tiny ginger girl waking up to grown men touching her inappropriately while trying to sleep. It was scary. Being so young, I had no idea what to do. Would my mom believe me? What would happen to my brother and me if we said anything? Am I supposed to enjoy this? Is this normal? So many questions ran through this little girl's head.

My brother and I ended up moving back to dad's house. My brother told our dad and stepmom that our stepbrother molested him and me. I confirmed that what he said was true. From then on, we were only allowed to go to our nana's house, and my biological mom had to visit us there. I never told about my stepdad molesting me until right before I turned 18 and became sexually active. I had flashbacks about what had happened and had to say something to save myself. I didn't want to because I was worried about how it would affect my biological mom, but I couldn't bear it any longer. I told my dad and stepmom about what had happened. I even told my biological mom, and she said, "*you need to learn to forgive and forget.*" I went to the advocacy center and explained to them what had happened. We even went to the police department where my biological mom and her husband lived to see if anything could be done. He was asked to take a polygraph test but declined. I felt that my biological mom took his side for so long. It hurt me. She stayed married to him until he got killed in a motorcycle accident.

I went to several years of counseling. My counselor was amazing. She helped me learn that it was not my fault. I am not a dirty person. I do matter. I will survive and prosper, and I WILL NOT let them win.

A couple of years went by, and I met my husband. We got married, and we had our first son within a year. During our marriage, I couldn't be intimate without having flashbacks. I couldn't think of things that had happened. I had no imagination for intimacy. It wasn't fair to me and wasn't fair to my husband.

Several years passed. My son, who was four years old, asked me if we could go to church. Crazy, right? He was so young. Well, I was moved by this. So guess what we did? We found a church. We found a really good church that opened up my eyes. They were so personable. They welcomed us like family. My heart was open and ready to serve the Lord. We ended up moving away from that area, and I lost touch with the church, the thing I needed in life that made me feel whole and worthy. I didn't stay in the Word, and life got busy.

In 2016, we moved to a little bitty town, Union City. My husband found a church that he wanted us to go to. He was not a church-goer, so it would be good to say he wanted us to attend this church. The church is impressive. We felt so welcomed. People came up left and right to meet and welcome us to the area. They have become our true family.

Fast-forward to August 2020. So much was going on. My biological mom said she was moving to Michigan. I had so many mixed feelings. Why now? I'm 34 years old; isn't it a bit late? I have kids, and I don't want them to get hurt. Am I going to trust her and her boyfriend? Around the same time, a friend asked me if I would share my testimony at a Stirred Up event. My first response was, *"I have never done that."* I wasn't sure if I could do that. That's a lot to share about yourself. Since I was younger, I have always said I would love to share my story with young girls so they could relate. I want them to know if they are going through any abuse, they do not need to fear telling. I don't want them to feel dirty. I don't want them to feel worthless. I prayed about it. I prayed for God to guide me. It was a few days later that I responded with YES! I will share my testimony.

In August 2020, my life was forever changed. I shared my story. I shared my pain, suffering, and heartache with many women I didn't know. I stood up in front of them with nothing written down. I had a big fear of speaking in front of people. I get very sweaty, shake and lose my words. I prayed for God to help me with my words, but I couldn't decide what I would write down. I didn't know that God had all of it planned for me.

When we got to the Stirred Up event, Bible verses were passed around. I took several of them and began to share my story. The Bible verses fit right in. It was like God was saying, I got you! I didn't stumble. The words just kept coming, and I wasn't afraid. I felt FREE! For the first time in my entire life, I felt so much lift off of my shoulders. I felt the chains break. I felt a new life come over me. Since that day, I have had a fire burning inside of me. I have shared with others without shame. I have not held back. I have been able to relate to women who have gone through similar experiences. I know this isn't all for me. I know that I will be able to touch more people each day.

When you meet me and think all those positive, uplifting, and happy things about me...I want you to know that wasn't always me, but it is now! I'm all about forgiveness. I'm a person who gives second chances. I'm someone who people can confide in. God's grace saves me. I'm not at all perfect. I fail too, but I keep going. I try to learn from my mistakes. Thank the good Lord above that I know I am worthy. The blood has cleansed me. I am not going to live in fear. I am not holding back. I am not going to let THEM win. I am going to make a change. I am going to help as many people as I can in life. No matter what it may be, I want to make a change. I want to make others feel happy and loved. I want to make them feel safe. I want to let them know that God loves them, and no matter how lonely they feel in this world, HE is there. HE loves us and will not forsake us. I am a mother to three amazing kiddos. I am a wife to an amazing husband who also knows the Lord. I am a Registered

Nurse. I am a God-loving woman. God has given me avenues to share His love, which I will continue to do!

"So do not fear, for I am with you; do not be dismayed, for I am your God. I will strengthen you and help you; I will uphold you with my righteous right hand" —Isaiah 41:10

JESSICA ZWENG

My name is Jessica Zweng. I was an LPN for 13 years and decided to return to school. I have been a Registered Nurse now for almost a year. I work at a long-term care facility as the Director of Nursing. I love the elderly and trying to make a difference in the workplace. I have been married for almost 17 years. We have two boys, 16, 13, and a girl, 5. I enjoy camping with my family, listening to worship music, and being outside watching our boys play baseball and football. I also like working out.

I love life to the fullest. Life can be so short, and we can't take it for granted. I encourage you to always look on the bright side and make at least one person smile daily.

On Nov 22, 1990, I surrendered my alcohol and drug addiction to the God of "my understanding." It began in adolescence, at the age of 12. I had used drugs and alcohol to escape the trauma of childhood physical abuse by a mentally ill older sibling, the familial chaos of 8 children, a dad that worked 16 hours a day, and a mom who, though at home, had an alcohol problem. The alcohol and drugs gave me a false sense of comfort, and I quickly learned to cope with my problems by escaping into the abyss of getting drunk and high. It was all a lie. It was a void that needed filling. It was a need that only God could fill.

I began a 31 1/2-year journey of sobriety and discovery, having met my personal Savior, Jesus, through a friend I met in AA. I would pray to God during early sobriety and ask Him for help. I knew Him, but I didn't *know* Him. By His grace and the invitation of a friend, I was invited to a Bible study where I heard the truth of the gospel for the first time. I heard that my alcohol and drug use were sin issues, that He loves me, that He died for me, and that I needed to ask Him to forgive my sins and trust Him alone for my eternal life. I always thought I had to do good things and earn my place in Heaven. At that Bible study, I asked Christ to be my Savior and to forgive me of my sin. I thought *it couldn't be that easy!* I had no idea what that meant, but I knew something had changed.

Since then, I have desired to know Him more intimately and love Him more fully. His Word is the foundation on which I have since built my life. He continues to bless me and sustain me. He has mercifully kept me from using alcohol and drugs, and He graciously reminds me that I am loved and cherished and one of His own. He has shown me that all things are possible through Him and that His grace is sufficient to live an abundant, joyful life in this broken world. I know now that no matter what, I am safe in His presence and assured of an eternal home with Him forever in Heaven.

"I have been crucified with Christ. It is no longer I who live, but Christ I lives in me, and the life which I now live in the flesh, I live by faith in the Son of God, who loves me, and gave Himself for me." —Galatians 2:20

JOANNE JOHNSTON

My name is Joanne Johnston. I grew up in Chicago and moved to Michigan in 2013, where I have lived ever since. I have worked in healthcare for over 30 years. I married my high school sweetheart, Pat, and we have been married for 39 years. We have four sons, a daughter-in-law, and a dog named Emmie. I love being with family and am well-known for my love of worship music.

It's on my heart to share with you a significant change that I underwent when I was 12 years old that ended up being one of the best experiences of my life.

In middle school, I dealt with a lot of bullying. This went on for years and continued to worsen with no end in sight. My family began to weigh our options of what we could do about the situation, and soon a family friend reached out with some information about a different school. I want to note that I was not on board with first switching schools. I had gone to the same school from kindergarten through sixth grade. Even though I was in a tough place, I didn't want to move because I feared the change. Not to mention I would be going from a small private school to a much larger public school.

I was ultimately against attending a public school solely from fear of the unknown. I procrastinated all summer on making a decision. We got to the point where I was enrolled in both my old and new school, and I didn't know where to go until right before the first day. Eventually, my transfer paperwork was approved, and my final decision was to move to my new school. This was a terrifying change for a 12-year-old who knew nothing different from where she had gone for her entire life, but it turned out to be one the best decisions I have ever made. I made friends quickly, and even though it was overwhelming initially, I've met some of the most amazing people I would have never known if I hadn't been willing to trust in the change. I went from being in a really tough place to making a decision that turned out to be better than I could have ever imagined. I am beyond blessed to have had some of the best experiences and opportunities due to this change. As I look back, I'm not sure what my life would look like if I hadn't been willing to step out in faith and embrace a change.

I want you to know that even if something seems intimidating and you feel you'd rather stay inside your comfort zone, God always has a plan. Getting out of your comfort zone is by no means easy, but sometimes it is the best thing to do. I would have stayed in an unhealthy environment if I hadn't trusted the Lord with my decision and gone through with it. I hope you feel encouraged to step out in faith, no matter what you face, and to trust God and His plan for you because you never know the amazing things He has in store.

JOY WOLF

Hey everyone! I'm Joy, and I am thrilled to have this opportunity to share a small part of my life with you! My interests include Spanish and ninja warrior, and I love working with kids. I hope you are encouraged and can take something away from my story.

If you were to look at my life from an outward perspective, you would probably view me as just a typical teenager trying to get through high school and figure out what she wants to do with her life. But something has always separated me from other kids my age: **my faith**. Sometimes I would even get made fun of because I don't swear or have certain morals. Most kids my age get caught up in worldly things just because other kids are doing it and because they are being told that it's alright to do things like that. I, however, am the total opposite!

You will probably find me at my house watching movies, listening to music, or hanging out with my family on a Friday night. I have always struggled making friends ever since elementary school. I have always felt "cursed" because I am naturally an introvert and struggle with anxiety. My parents have always said I was timid, even at a young age. Whether being deathly afraid of the Chuck E. Cheese mascot or even simple things like jumping out of the car, these things still carry with me today in different ways.

Recently, I went through a very dark couple of months where my anxiety was probably at its worst. There were days when I would have multiple breakdowns a day, and all I wanted to do was to lay down and go to sleep just so the day would be over. I would miss countless class periods or even the day, and if I did go to school, I would go with swollen eyes and tear stains. I would always make up some lame excuses every time people asked me where I was or why I left; I didn't want anybody to ever see me like that. Honestly, I hadn't dealt with anything this extreme before, so I had no idea what to do or what was going on. The anxiety started affecting me physically, and I felt like losing my mind.

One day, I decided that I needed to do something to change this. The Devil was coming; he was already in my mind controlling me. He was coming to take my name and spirit away from God, and his grip was not loosening. I realized that I had done nothing to fight back. I wasn't building a connection with God. I wasn't letting Him in to help me. So I decided that I was going to write a personal letter to God and hang it up on my wall. It said that I was thankful that God let me go through this season of life because it only strengthened me.

I told Him that I would stay faithful to God no matter what. Almost every time I doubted, I would read that letter on my wall. I was also led to writing different Scriptures on sticky notes to carry around. My favorite one was 2 Timothy 1:7,

"For the Spirit God gave us does not make us timid, but gives us power, love, and self-discipline."

I would carry it around in my school laptop case and take it out to read it whenever I felt anxious. Eventually, I got out of that dark mindset, and I am now starting to think more positively and trying to set aside time for God consistently. But that doesn't mean I now don't struggle with my anxiety. Some days it's terrible, and some days it's bearable, but I have learned over the past few months that I still need to strive to get that connection with God no matter what state I'm in.

To do that, I recently decided to get baptized at my church. I felt that God was telling me it was time to take a step closer to Him and let Him take control. I had decided to do it last minute, and the enemy did not want me to do it. He filled me with fear and anxiety, but I told God I was committing, and I did it. I wasn't going to let the Devil step in front of me, even if I was too scared to speak in front of people and tell them my testimony!

As I go about life now, I realize how many kids face the same problems I deal with, and I never want anyone to be stuck sitting with the Devil. I want to help them get out. I once heard that God is always with us, whether we know it or not. So that means that if God is with us, then everywhere we go is considered Holy Ground. We are standing on Holy Ground, and we cannot let the lies of the Devil stand on that ground. He doesn't belong there, which is why we need to fight back and look at the truth, which is God. Studies say that fear is one of the strongest emotions, but if people have just the tiniest bit of hope, it surpasses fear.

There has been one quote that has stuck out to me recently. It says, *"Hope is the only thing stronger than fear. A little hope is effective. A lot of hope is*

112

dangerous." I put this in my perspective on my relationship with God. He is my hope in these situations, and when fear seems to be the only thing standing in my life, He always comes out bigger than my fear. The more you put hope (God) into your life, the more dangerous it is for the Devil to stand his ground.

MADELYNN PAYNE

Madelynn Payne is a 17-year-old Senior at Union City High School. She plans to graduate and hopefully attend a university but has yet to decide what she will study. She is the oldest child in a family of six, with two younger brothers and a younger sister. Her Dad is the pastor at Union City Assembly of God, so she has been exposed to Christianity her whole life. She hopes her walk with God will become stronger every day and to influence kids her age with her story so far!

It was a brisk winter morning some 30 years ago—freshly fallen snow, children sleeping, the Christmas season, and entertaining a guest.

My husband and I had given our bedroom to our guest, and we were sleeping on a hideaway bed (remember those?) in the living room. We arose that morning, and I began preparing for work and the day. I was all ready to go except for shoes. I proceeded to the bedroom to grab a pair, and an image was embedded in my mind today! My husband was embracing another woman (our guest) in *my bed*! Da-ja-Vu! Not again! You see...I'd been in this same situation eight years earlier with a newborn. Now there were two precious ones to consider and care for.

I went to work and tried to stay focused on my class that day. I came home to an empty house.

I grabbed a dish towel off the counter and fell to my knees in a crumbled heap, sobbing uncontrollably in the middle of the kitchen. Emotions whirling...hurt, crushed, angry, confused, spent. I kinda pulled it together and did the only thing I knew to do...I cried out to God! I told Him I was at a crossroads...I could throw in the towel and say..."*Look where serving God has gotten me!*" OR "*I choose to hold TIGHT to your hand!*".

I lifted my hands toward heaven and cried..."*God, I'm choosing to hold tight to Your hand!*"

The journey wasn't easy! We had to leave the church we were pastoring, leave all our wonderful friends, and move back to a very unfinished and needy home.

The kids and I walked in...I was emotionally overwhelmed. They ran upstairs as I sat down on a stool, wondering how in the world can I do this. How can I stay here? I thought there was just now way!

Just then, the kids came back downstairs, so excited to be home. You see, we'd only been gone six months. At that very moment, God said, "*This is where you need to be!*"

Sunday rolled around, and during worship, I envisioned myself in a tube, stretching from the floor to the throne room of Heaven, isolated from the whole world. Just me and Jesus! I raised my hands and began to PRAISE HIM! God truly inhabits the praises of His people!

After service, a woman approached me and asked, *"How can you praise God?"*. My reply..., *"How can I not?"* Praising Jesus sheds new light on things. Circumstances don't look so impossible. Praising Him brings hope, life, and joy. It brings peace that passes ALL understanding.

God miraculously provided ALL of our needs...from windows to carpet to paint, a new job, and precious friends. His supply is endless. He even granted some of our heart's desires.

Choosing Jesus is NEVER a mistake! He NEVER fails! If you glean anything from my story, learn this...ALWAYS choose Jesus! No matter your circumstances or how bad things appear...keep your eyes on HIM! He is BIGGER and BETTER than anything!

God is MORE than enough and ALL that we need!

DEBBIE DRAKE

I love to care for the elderly, and I enjoy making homemade cards. I enjoy being outside in my flower garden. But most of all, I love sharing Jesus whenever and wherever possible. He's my best friend!

Being a PK doesn't necessarily mean you have a relationship with Jesus; having a "title" doesn't mean you've surrendered your heart to Him.

As a young (tween) believer, I didn't understand the importance of being rooted in the Word. I didn't understand the power of the spoken Word or how to apply it to my life. I never knew that it rained on the just and the unjust or that death was a part of life. All I knew was how a "good God" could allow bad things to happen to good people.

My faith was shaken after my mother died. When my father passed away some years later, I was so devastated that I lost my faith. My young mind had so many unanswered questions. As far as I was concerned, my parents were good deed-doers— humble and simple people who always went the extra mile in ministry, sometimes at our expense.

The pain was so deep and overwhelming that I couldn't bear it alone. I was stuck and couldn't process the grief and separation caused by mourning. The enemy knew this was my weakness and used it against me. Eventually, that sadness turned to anger and bitterness, which ultimately paved the way to atheism. I hated God, the church, and the ministry. In short, I had fallen for a lie. A very expensive lie that cost me many years of unnecessary despair and sorrow.

Looking back, I now see that the Lord kept me and protected me from myself. Over time, life's circumstances and poor choices led me back to the altar I had been savagely running from for decades. I came to Jesus broken, damaged, and hopeless. Amazingly, the Lord met my brokenness at that altar with such a powerful and transforming love that my life has never been the same. I was a prodigal.

I'm so thankful that my mother was a woman of prayer. I believe it was her prayers that reached me when I was far from the Lord. She's been gone for more than half of my life, but her prayers still echo to a faithful God in eternity.

RAQUELL MEDRANO SAIYED

Rev. Raquell Medrano Saiyed is a Licensed Minister at Iglesia del Espíritu Santo Ministries (IDES), where she leads the IDES Breakthrough Liturgical Dance Ministry and IDES Intercessor Ministry. In addition, she has been a Licensed Minister with Ephesians 4 Network for over ten years. In mid-2011, she became Assistant WIN/Prayer Director for E4N. She has a strong passion for the lost and has actively worked in prison ministry in the past.

The youngest Pastor's Kid of 9 children, Raquell, has experienced loss, depression, addiction, poverty, and illness. On Friday, September 13, 2002, she collided with the love of Jesus and has forever been changed. She is a living testimony of God's redeeming power to free the captives, heal the sick, bind the brokenhearted and give sight to the blind.

The Lord has given Raquell Isaiah 54; a promise and vision for her ministry. In October 2010, she birthed a prayer ministry in her home. This prayer ministry has grown into the IDES Prayer Network and IDES Ministry Of Intercession and crosses cultural and racial boundaries in the US and Mexico.

She believes that no matter where you've been, what you've done, or where you walked, God still has a plan and future for you! She believes this because she has experienced this in her own life. She enjoys spending time with her family and her two dogs, Patches, and Macy.

My family did not attend church, but occasionally I would go to church camp and youth groups throughout my teenage years. When I graduated high school and went to college in 2011, I spent eight years seeking acceptance in everything but the Lord. I had a full-ride scholarship for Interior Design, so when I was not doing homework or working, I looked for attention from boys. I thought my worth came from being in a relationship. I was always worried about finding my true love whom I would marry one day. This only caused anxiety and even depression because I felt unloved when guys didn't want to pursue serious relationships or would cheat on me while we dated.

I never struggled with drugs or alcohol. Instead, sex was my vice. After I had completed my master's degree, I found myself in a toxic job where my boss told me I would never make it in this world as an interior designer or architect. I went home to my toxic relationship that night, where my boyfriend had nothing good to say to me at the time. So, that night in October of 2018, I decided that if everything I had worked so hard for over the last eight years of school wasn't going to work out for me and my boyfriend didn't love me anymore, my life would not be worth it. I attempted suicide that night, and by the grace of God, I now have a second chance at life.

After getting my life back on track, I ended this relationship and left that job. I still struggled to find myself and continued seeking men and relationships. Luckily, my ex is the reason I came to Firm Foundation Ministries in Centreville, Michigan. I now call this church my home. In January 2021, I was saved as I came to know why Jesus died for me. On April 13th, 2021, I was baptized in the St. Joseph River to publicly declare the inward changes I had made in my heart by accepting Jesus Christ as my Lord and Savior.

Last fall, I also started E.D.G.E Bible College to pursue a bachelor's degree in Biblical Studies. During this time, I was doing online Bible studies where I also got to know my now fiancé. The first conversation I had with Jon when things started moving towards courtship and dating was, "I do see you as someone I could pursue life with, but I want you to know I struggle with sexual sin. I promised God the night I was baptized to save myself for my husband." Jon was very respectful and said he would honor this in our relationship.

I spent most of 2021 single, praying to God, asking him for my husband. I remember God telling me, "If you can't love yourself enough and love Me, how can you love your husband?" And God was right! I worked on my mental health and relationship with the Lord for eight months before meeting Jon. I am so thankful to have met my future husband and to know God put him in my life for a reason. Jon and I have been dating since November 24th, 2021. Jon proposed to me on March 11th, 2022, and we plan to get married on November 11th, 2022.

God knew I needed to go through the hard break-ups and lessons I learned by dating men who were not good for me. He also knew finding my "dream career" and buying my "dream jeep" would not fulfill the emptiness in my heart; only Jesus could fill the hole I had in my heart.

BRITTANY JAE

Brittany is an Interior Designer & Architectural Designer. She is an Organizational Leader for Howardsville 4-H club and Rabbit Assistant Superintendent for St. Joseph County Grange Fair.

Brittany attended Firm Foundation Ministries in Centreville, MI, and was baptized on April 13, 2021. She has a three-year-old Black Lab named Bella. She named her after Ciao Bella greeting from when she lived in Italy. She loves taking Bella for rides in her jeep, traveling, finding waterfalls, and hiking in the mountains. Her dream is to travel to all 50 states before age of 50!

Brittany is engaged to the most patient man she's ever met, Jon, and will get married on November 11, 2022!

I once knew a little girl who had an incredible light on her life. Her joy was tangible, her laughter contagious. Her world was filled with promise.

Then one day, this blonde, curly-headed little girl watched her parents divorce, and her light grew a little dimmer.

The years ahead would not be like before. There would be times when she would try to take her breath away.

When she was very young, she was sexually abused by a man near and dear to her. She told no one, but again her light grew a little dimmer.

That abuse broke something inside her, like a toy that's easily over-tightened and breaks into pieces, but no one sees it.

Her mother loved the Lord and took her to church. That would become the safe place after her life was shaken when she lost her dad. There she found solid ground. A place to count on. It felt stable. She struggled with acceptance after her dad left. As most young ones, she thought she wasn't good enough, or he would have stayed. In church, she found that acceptance. But, when you're broken on the inside, you are still constantly searching for that unconditional acceptance and love.

When she was 13, she found herself alone in a stairwell with an older man she had grown to look up to, searching for that fatherly love. Her heart longed for that father figure. She extended her heart...but he only wanted to take a piece of her soul. He was an abuser. Once again, her light grew a little dimmer.

She began to believe that her only worth was tied to her body. And by example, the only thing she had to offer was giving herself away...one piece at a time.

Dimmer...and dimmer.

Over the next several years, her life would unfold in teen pregnancy, one failed marriage after another, one where she would flee for her life with her three kids from a man who swore he would kill them all. At this point, she could no longer find her light at all. Her light would go out completely that day. Her insides grew dark. It seemed there was no place else to turn.

Through the years, she had known of God. She knew all of the Christianese...all the right things, but she never really knew Him.

Broken and beaten down, she came to His feet, crumbling in tears. "Jesus, I need You."

Not only did Jesus see her, but He scooped her up into His lap and held her close. He seemed to love her anyway, despite her brokenness.

From that day forward, one day at a time, piece by piece, her new love, this man of courage...her new best friend, began to heal every broken piece on the inside of her completely. He began to turn the dimmer switch of her life back in the opposite direction. He gave her light again.

You see, every piece taken from her was restored tenfold. He kept every tear she'd ever cried in a bottle, and when she was ready, He returned them to her.

Except for this time, He held them in His hand, turned them into oil, and anointed her life with them. And now, He would use her to carry that oil to put in the lamps of others whose lights had also grown dim or been taken from them.

Now a grown woman with a light brighter than she'd ever had, only because of a real Savior, walks in the victory. And though her sins are gone, she carries the memory, but not the hurt, of that sorted past.

Only to reach those who need to know that there is grace and forgiveness. No matter how bad you think, you are...No, matter how dark it is...THERE IS JESUS. And His grace can handle all of your weaknesses.

You need but bring it to His feet, like I did.

For that little girl was me.

"Each time, He said, "My grace is all you need. My power works best in weakness." So now I am glad to boast about my weaknesses so that the power of Christ can work through me." —2 Corinthians 12:9

STEPHANIE PALMER

Stephanie Palmer is a woman with a heart that runs after God and the things of Him. In truth, nothing else matters.

Her life changed after she was introduced to Jesus Christ as a child. She suffered abuse early on and searched for her true identity in Christ. Once she realized who she was and what she was, she refused to let go.

In recent years, she has felt the call of God on her life to step into ministry through sharing prophetic dreams, writing, singing, and speaking. She is pursuing His will as to what that looks like next.

She has a heart for the broken because she knows what it is to be broken and redeemed. She is the mother of three grown kids and runs an office for a family-owned business in Houston, Texas.

She is always asking herself, "What next, God"?

After I graduated from college, I ended up working a comfortable job. I wasn't growing, and I wasn't being challenged at work. That was okay for a while, but after a couple of years, I started to feel bothered that I wasn't progressing where I was. Additionally, the job took up all my time, so I never had time for friends, family, or fun; I was miserable. I value my friends and family more than anything, so this was painful. The pain I was feeling was the starting point for lasting change. At the time, I felt helpless to change my circumstances. I wanted to leave my job, but I felt stuck. It was a secure and steady job, so I didn't just want to up and leave no matter how much I wanted to. So, I did the next best thing. I couldn't change my circumstances, so I started to work on myself.

I began to read self-improvement books, read my Bible more often, watch motivational videos, and listen to sermons. I was growing personally, professionally, and of course, spiritually. I got into the habit of feeding my mind daily with the Word of God and something educational. Even though my circumstances didn't change, I still showed up daily; I was walking by faith. The first book I read on my journey was *'Atomic Habits'* by James Clear. This book helped me change my perspective, break bad habits and build healthier ones. The book also encouraged me to start a blog and share my journey with others.

Writing about my journey helped me grow and transform for the better. I began to understand myself more deeply as I wrote about what I was learning on my journey. I felt like God put it on my heart to start a blog and gave me the strength and courage to write the articles I'd written.

"For God has not given us the spirit of fear, but of power, and of love, and of a sound mind." —2 Timothy 1:7

One of my worst habits was that I focused too much on fear. My mind would always go to what could go wrong, what I couldn't do, what I didn't have, the fear of starting, the fear of failing, and so forth. While on my growth journey, I grew closer to God and deepened my faith, giving me a whole new perspective on life. I started cultivating gratitude, which helped me appreciate life more. I also started to choose faith over fear by feeding my mind daily with the Word of God. This allowed me to transform my mind and be free from the negative emotions dominating my life. I found comfort, courage, and strength in reading and listening to the Word of God.

God set me free from several destructive patterns that kept me stuck in life. I am so grateful for His grace and mercy. Throughout my growth journey, God has led and guided me. I'm excited about God's plan for my life. I'm still learning and growing daily, and I'm confident God is with me.

ABIMBOLA JUBRIL

Hi, my name is Abimbola Jubril, and I'm from Portage, Michigan. I enjoy writing, learning, reading, and spending time with friends and family.

Follow me on my journey of growth. Check out my blog abimbolajubril.com.

As I sat with my steaming cup of coffee, the fresh smell of pumpkin filled the air and took me back (carried me back) to some amazing memories and some not-so-amazing. As my mind drifted from this life I now live into the distant memory of another life I once lived, I stopped, and I thanked God for His protection...not just a few times, but over and over again. Contemplating this journey (you know, the one called life), I was reminded of His word, which says:

"For here is what the Lord has spoken to me: Because you have delighted in Me as My great lover, I will greatly protect you. I will set you in a high place, safe and secure before My face. I will answer your cry for help every time you pray." —Psalm 91:14 & 15 (TPT)

There I was...five hours from home, thinking I was going to spend an intimate weekend working on my broken marriage. I was broken by lies, abuse, pornography, drugs, and adultery. But I forgive, right? Seventy times seven, right? I've gotta give it another shot....

But now, I am sitting in a pickup truck down a small two-track in the middle of the woods, somewhere, with the fresh smell of bonfire smoke and the pungent smell of evil accompanied by satanic music booming into the night air.

"Get out of the truck."

"No," I said. *"It's evil here, and I'm not getting out."*

"Suit yourself," he said, accompanied by a vast array of other colorful language spewing and muttering as he walked away.

So, I sat in the middle of evil under a dark sky, doors locked, not knowing exactly where I was but praying to God that He would keep me safe. Two hours later, he jumped in the truck and peeled out of that muddy two-track, taking me to an abandoned trailer with no electricity, running water, and phone service (an old hunting camp). I went to bed that night, praying I would return home to my beautiful girls, realizing I still had two more days to endure.

The following day when I woke up, I stepped outside to use the luxurious "outhouse" a short distance away with weeds taller than me! As I was beginning to head back, I looked up, and he was standing in the doorway, staring at me. He said, *"Huh, I could have shot you in the back, and no one would ever know."*

COMPLETE SHOCK-PARALYZED as those words pierced my heart, mind, and soul forever...I knew...I might not make it.

But GOD had a different plan for me under the feathers of His wings. I was safe and tucked away with the wisdom not to speak, question, or cause dangerous escalation. And that was the beginning of the end, which was a new beginning! Even though my first husband passed away in a terrible accident and ten years later, a plot was revealed about an attempt to end my life with one of his friends (who also passed), I left behind that scary night and all that was attached to it. I left the broken commitment long before I saw the truth. God saved me physically, mentally, emotionally, and spiritually from that time forward (sometimes three steps forward and two steps back) but forward...

Enthroned under the shadow of Shaddai. Hidden in the strength of God Most High.

He will be my glorious hero and give me a feast, and I will be satisfied with a full life and all He does for me.

I will surely enjoy the fullness of my salvation and the sweet time with Him every day, accompanied by my new life and the many smells of Home in my coffee cup.

DAWN LENO

Dawn is a passionate worship leader from Michigan (a musician and artist/teacher) and has been leading in various capacities for 14 years. Although she began speaking about worship and leading later in life (in the latter years of raising a family), she is no less zealous or tired of the amazing things that God can and is doing through singing, playing, and writing worship music. The Lord is looking for true worshipers who worship in Spirit and Truth!

My earliest childhood memories were of living in a big, old farmhouse. I had a huge playroom with lots of toys and many dolls. Often you would see me lugging around a doll or cat in my tiny little arms or pushing them around in my toy stroller. I also remember the many tea parties and picnics I would have with my cat, **Dusty**. Those were the happiest memories of my childhood.

Those pleasant memories soon became few and far between once I attended elementary school. It was as if all fun had ended, and fear erupted. At Kindergarten Round-Up, it was discovered that I had a vision issue with my left eye. Due to the vision issues, I had to wear glasses and a patch over the Lazy-eye. That alone was enough to deal with, as I remember the other children always staring at me and poking at my eye patch. That was nothing compared to the fear I experienced riding the bus. I remember feeling so tiny waiting for the big yellow school bus to come down the road to pick me up.

For the first week of school, I would cry every morning because I was so scared to get on the bus. So many disturbing thoughts and unanswered questions would race through my mind...*How will I find my classroom once I get to school? What if I get lost and can't find my way home? How will I find my bus once school is over and it's time to go home?* Unfortunately, at such a young age, I could not fully articulate the disturbing feeling that I was experiencing to my parents in a way they would understand. They just thought I was "a baby" and threatened to spank me if I didn't stop crying. I did stop crying on the outside, but not on the inside. It was as if an overwhelming sense of fear and dread would invade my mind and emotions. It was tough for me to focus, especially at school.

From Kindergarten to sixth grade, the fear and anxiety escalated in me. My family and I moved several times, which meant different attending schools. I struggled academically, so by 3rd grade, I had to leave my regular classroom daily for the "Resource Class" to get exceptional help with reading and math. This was humiliating and degrading to me. The negative thoughts in my mind through these years were continual...*What's wrong with me? Am I stupid? Will I ever make it in life? Why are things so hard for me to understand? Why can't I be like other kids my age?* To my knowledge, I was never diagnosed with any particular learning disabilities. It seemed that I had extreme difficulty processing and retaining information, though. However, I believe the fear and confusion that plagued my mind blocked my ability to concentrate and focus.

Also, some adverse incidents in third and one 5th grade still stand out to me. In third grade, the teacher gave us timed math drills. We were to complete as many math problems before the timer went off, and then we were to switch papers and grade each other's papers. I did not complete my paper, and every sum I did calculate was incorrect. I still remember how humiliating it was to me. The girl, who graded my paper, took it to every student in the class and showed them I had failed. I remember running into the bathroom with tears streaming down my face, feeling rejected and degraded. Another time in this same class, I wore a wig to school because my aunt cut my hair too short. I remember looking into the mirror after she had cut it and thinking how ugly it looked and that the kids at school would make fun of me and say I looked like a boy. My mom said I could wear a wig to school if I didn't like it. She bought me a wig, and I wore it for a few days until the kids and teacher realized I was wearing it. One boy in the class pulled it off my head after recess and ran around with it, making fun of me. I don't remember crying in the bathroom, but I do remember wanting to go home and wishing I'd never have to return.

The other terrifying situation I want to highlight is when I was a fifth grader. We lived on a dirt road in the country. The school district wouldn't allow the bus driver to turn down our road to pick me up, so I had to walk a mile down the country dirt road to get to the bus stop. It was fine when my brother walked with me; however, once I was a fifth grader, he was in junior high and took a different bus and went in the other direction. That meant I had to walk the mile down the dirt road alone. My aunt, who cut my hair, just randomly asked me one day if I was scared of kidnappers. She said they drive by, cut little kids into pieces, and throw them into ditches. For some reason, I never questioned her. I believed it to be true...like it just happened every day in the neighborhood, and I had better watch out! The thought of that caused more fear and torment in me. Walking that road was terrifying every morning, and the fear carried over into my school day. For a long time, I never shared what she told me with anyone. I just lived in fear. I would run in the ditches behind the trees instead of walking on the road to the bus stop. Every time a car would drive by, I would feel my heart pounding. When I got to the bus stop, I was worn out and exhausted from the fear and running. It finally got to me, and I started crying at school.

My teacher eventually called my mother. I finally told her why I was crying. She did make arrangements to pick me up, so I didn't have to walk the dirt road anymore. These were just a few of the many struggles and challenges academically and emotionally during those early years.

Some good happened during those years, too. Often my grandparents or aunts and uncles would take my brother and me to Sunday school and church. It was in church that I learned that Jesus loves me. It was one positive thing I believed. Knowing that "Jesus loved me" gave me comfort and hope. It sparked the encouragement I needed to press through those difficult times

When I was in fourth grade, my parents separated and eventually got a divorce. They both remarried a few years later, which brought more change and uncertainty, as well as another move and a new school.

JODY WING

Jody is the daughter of the one true King, wife, mother, prayer warrior, animal lover, entrepreneur, rock painter, hiker, and home girl.

Jody is the leader and facilitator of the It Is Well Group/Table at Kfirst in Portage, MI. She desires to help women of all ages gain a deeper understanding of who they are in Christ, hear and discern God's voice, and support one another. As we do this, His plans and purposes for us unfold. We step into our destiny and calling. Together we are stronger and more courageous!

You can connect with Jody in the It Is Well Women's/Prayer Connect Facebook Group.

I was born into a pastor's family. Even though I had a great family, I still had sexual abuse from a neighbor. God allowed me to block it until I was old enough to heal. Now He uses me to heal others through a process called Sozo.

When I was in Ministry School, a man came to our church and prayed for the amygdala (My Memory Center, the almond-shaped thing at the back of my neck that holds the memories, good and bad). I was slain in the spirit, and while I was on the ground, the Lord told me I would be out of counseling and start losing weight just by soaking in the presence of God. I had lost twenty-five pounds and was counseling my counselor by the end of the month. I lost eighty-five pounds in six months just by soaking.

We had to take a trip to the Dominican Republic during Ministry School. While there, we prayed for the sick. I prayed for a man in a wheelchair for twenty years, with one leg about a foot shorter than the other. The doctor said he would never walk again. I prayed that his back would be even and his leg would start growing. The other fifteen students were also praying, and then one gal said, *"let's stand him up."* She and I helped him walk, and then he started walking alone. Praise the Lord! Then there was a lady who spoke only Spanish, and I knew she was deaf in one ear. The Lord told me to keep praying, and I said, *"out of the warehouse in heaven, I access a new eardrum because that's what God said it was."* After about fifteen minutes, she started crying as I clicked my fingers, and she could hear me. God had done that miraculous thing!

God is still the same in the States. The same power is here to heal if you only believe that Jesus has done the work. I'm a family pastor at our church, and when people come up to get prayed for, they get healed of mental, physical, spiritual, and financial issues. God gave one lady a new knee. So many miracles for others and myself. God is still in the miracle-working business!

KAREN OGDEN

I ran from the idea of being in ministry until my head pastor persuaded me to go on my first mission trip, and I was hooked. Years later, our church started the School of Supernatural Ministry. My passion is to see people saved, healed, and delivered, mind, soul, and body, as well as know their identity in Christ and walk in their God-given destinies.

When you think of joy, what comes to mind? Do you think of smiling and laughter? Often, people think of the emotion of happiness. Happiness states that your situation must benefit you, and you will feel happy. However, joy isn't dependent on a situation. Joy isn't an emotion but rather a choice.

If you ask any of my family members, coworkers, or people at church, they will say I am joyful. However, most people don't know I have 24/7 migraines and body pain. I learned the secret to finding joy, even while suffering. But first, let's back up to when it all started.

Back in early 2019, I began having sporadic headaches. By the summer, they were frequent enough that my pediatrician recommended seeing a neurologist. The neurologist declared that I had migraines. She then prescribed some magnesium and other vitamins to help prevent them. However, fast forward three months, and I had them 2-3 times per week. At the next neurologist appointment, she changed my diagnosis to chronic migraines. During this time, I started to have random body pains. In early 2020, my migraines became 24/7. Since then, we have gone to various specialties and have tried all different types of meds. We have tried Botox, physical therapy, and even chiropractic care. Over 15 neurologists have seen me, and each one has been stumped. As the years have gone on, the pain has worsened, and I now have chronic body pain. I also have many other symptoms, ranging from nausea to seizure-like spasms to vertigo to numbness. However, even during suffering, I have been able to have joy.

James 1:2 states,

Consider it pure joy, my brothers and sisters, whenever you face trials of many kinds.

When I first read this verse, I was confused. Why should I consider it a joy when I am suffering? Maybe for you today, it isn't a sickness you're facing. Maybe you're facing job loss, depression, or relationship struggles. Most people stop after the second verse, but to understand what God means, we must look at the second verse. James 1:3 states, *"because you know that the testing of your faith produces perseverance."* God is showing us that it isn't for nothing when we face suffering. Rather, as we face difficulty, our faith is strengthened. God works for the good in every situation. Even if we don't see God working, He is still there with us every step of the way. The secret to finding joy even in the trials of life is choosing to wait on God. Waiting on God means being willing to give Him control of the situation. It is learning to have faith that He has a plan and that it is good. As we make this choice, we are choosing the joy of the Lord to be our strength. As we choose joy, we begin to develop greater faith and strength. This allows us to stand firm in our faith as we face the trials of this world.

As I have gone through this journey, God always brings to mind a verse. That verse is Isaiah 40:31a. It states, *"But they that wait upon the Lord shall renew their strength."* When we wait on God, He will give us the strength needed to go through the trials of life. True joy comes when we wait on God and choose to have faith in Him, no matter what we go through. Only then will we be able to have joy in every circumstance.

Today, I want to encourage you to examine your own life. What struggles are you facing? Have you given God control of your situation? As you wait on God, allow your faith to grow. Depend on Him as the source of your strength. Remember that true joy comes from God alone. And be encouraged that God is always with you, no matter what you face in this life.

HANNAH ELSTON

Hannah is a senior in high school. She lives in Holland, Michigan, with her parents and two sisters. She loves watching football and cheering on her favorite team, the Michigan Wolverines. She loves shopping at Hobby Lobby, baking delicious treats, and reading the latest book. Hannah has a heart for helping the chronically/ terminally ill to discover God's goodness and faithfulness amid their circumstances.

The Lord captured my heart at a young age, and communicating my testimony seems indifferent. We have all heard miraculous stories about being saved from addictions or unbelief, so these obvious moments of repentance left me questioning how I could tell others my story. Although infidelity, divorce, remarriage, financial issues, addictions, and insecurities were a part of my family's story, I would not describe my childhood as bad. God grew my gifts through our family dynamics, my environment, and my position as the oldest of 9 children. We can easily become victims of our circumstances, but God gives us the strength to be victors!

Since my parents did not attend church then, I remember sitting on the front porch of my mom's new Leer Street house as a little girl, waiting on my great-aunt Rere to pick me up for church in her big gray Buick. I would spend other weekends with her and my Granny at our church's widows' home, Peace Manor, and my cousin and I would ride the church bus together with a group of the sweet widow. God used this place and those women to cultivate a desire to be in church. Peace Manor and the church building became my safe place. However, I could not be at all four church services we had each week, so sometimes, I felt left out.

Most girls my age had their parents in church and a very close bond. These were the girls who always had cute church outfits and were picked for the solos in the Sunshine Choir. I did not have dresses like that. I couldn't sing. Besides that, they were the ABCs (Amber, Brittany, Courtenay, and Sarah), and my name was Erica - just one letter off. They were not mean girls, and they did not exclude me; they just had grown up together. It's only natural I felt a little inadequate.

One day, at about the age of 12, I was standing at our church usher's window, and a little girl named Tiah came up to me and said, "*I want to be just like you when I grow up!*" My restricted thought was, "*Who is me? You got the wrong girl. I am an E - not an A, B, C's, not even a D!*" As she looked into my eyes, I knew she was talking to me. That moment of her seeing me changed my perspective of myself. I was an instant role model, and she wanted to continue to be someone she could look up to. This little girl "seeing me" was like Jesus saying, "*I see you, and I want others to see me in you.*" My story, like yours, has moments of hurt, struggle, anger, unfaithfulness, forgiveness, joy, and victory, but this snapshot of a little girl's impact on my life I share with you today has shaped my life's mission to say *"I see you"* just like "Jesus sees you." When you finally realize that Jesus sees you, for me, it was through a little girl; you have no other choice but to help others know that He sees them too. We have the power to communicate *"Because Jesus saw me. I see you."* Let Jesus in you translate to Jesus in them. It's that simple.

ERICA COOK

Erica Cook is the oldest of a blended family of 9 children. In 1999, she married her husband Peter and began college at Tri-State University in Angola, IN, where she received her bachelor's in elementary education. Peter and Erica together have two children, Luci and Levi, and she loves being a mom and supporting them in their passions. Beyond her children, she loves building relationships with other children. Erica and her husband own and operate Cook's Bison Ranch; their family business started just several months before they married in December 1998. Together they host multiple groups at their ranch every year to share their story and love for bison. Outside the bison industry, Erica serves on staff at her local church, enjoys being involved in her community, looks for ways to use her gifts to serve others, and loves connecting and bringing people together. Her greatest desire is for people to know Jesus and experience the power of being in His presence.

Called To A Higher Place

The raindrops slowly rolled down the small window in my bedroom. I stared past the rain at the house next door. The small addition I found myself in did not feel like home. I was miles away from the people I loved and cherished most. I felt stuck in my life season and my walk with the Lord. Tears began to roll down my cheeks, mimicking the rhythm of the rain on the window. I cried to God, "please hear me" I begged, "I know you called me to this place, but I have no idea why." Silence met my cries. I slowly curled up in a ball on my bedroom floor, letting the sobs escape my body.

I began to let the memories of the years replay in my mind. Fear, failure, difficult ministry experiences, manipulation, spiritual abuse, and the death of those I held dear. The sobs kept coming as despair overcame me. I lay in that place of darkness for what seemed like hours. Then slowly but surely, a slight glimmer of light began to shine into my heart as I began to allow the memories of the faithfulness of God to fill my mind. The memories of triumph and victory began to trump the fear. I remembered how God had used me in ministry as those in the dark walked into the light. The relationships in my life bloomed because of the presence of God. The beauty that came out of the ashes of abuse. Hope began to rise as my breathing slowed.

I uncurled my body from a ball on the floor to kneeling. "I trust You, I trust You, You are faithful, not my will but Yours." As the words continued to flow from my lips, a peaceful flow of the presence of God rushed into that small bedroom. His sweet presence wrapped around me like a hug. "I have never left you." The words brought life to my bones. "Look over your life; celebrate My faithfulness. I have done great things in your life before, and I will do it again, not because of what you can give Me but because of your willingness to surrender your will for Mine. I am the Beginning and the End, the Alpha and the Omega."

Tears began to fall from my eyes again, but they were tears of thanksgiving and joy this time. I felt the sweet embrace of the Lord as I pondered the spirit of despair and self-pity that the enemy tries to trap us in. He desperately wants to get us to a place of fear and isolation so we feel like we are the only ones battling. God brings us to a place of freedom through His words and His presence. As we grasp this identity that God has called us to live in, it starts with coming to a higher place with Him and reminding ourselves of the faithfulness of God.

God has also called us to live in a community that can challenge us when we fall into despair and encourages us to run the race and live in the calling of God. We get one life, and often hours, days, and weeks get wasted on thoughts that are lies and deception. I have fallen into the trap, and God rescued me with His loving hand. God has called us to a life of intentionality, time spent in His presence seeking His face. We are called to a higher place of intimacy and a higher place of rest, resisting the enemy's schemes and entering into the promise of God.

If you are in a season where you feel stuck, know you are not alone. Look around and identify God's people in your life for a time like this. Lean into them with vulnerability and truth about your season. Let them love you. Next, remember this is just a season; it will end. That said, run straight into what you are facing with eyes wide open, willing to see and embrace what God is trying to teach you. Often that lesson consists of entering into a place of surrender and understanding that, no matter what, God is good and deserves to be praised. Paul understood trials and the heart of God when he said in James 1, *"Count it ALL joy."*

The victory is HIS, and He shares it with us. So embrace the One who has the answers, live in obedience, and surrender your will for His. I promise, friend, you will move past this season and into a season of abundance. Regardless, in both seasons, you will find peace in Him. I now find myself in a place that feels like home, surrounded by those I love, finding rest in the chaos and answers in the unknown. I attribute that to the God who called me to a higher place. So run the race with endurance, find Him, embrace Him, and never let go!

ANNA PRANGER

Anna Pranger is the Founder of Stirred Up Ministries. She travels and speaks at conferences, churches, coffee shops, and in-home gatherings, sharing truth through the prophetic gifting of the Holy Spirit. Anna desires to inspire others to operate in the truth of who God truly is, limitless and not confined by the boxes we put Him in.

Anna's heart is for the chains of religion to be bound and for grace to be loosed in the souls of those who desire freedom. She is the author of profound books that take you on a journey to discover the Trinity and find your true self along the way.

Find her books and other resources at www.stirredupministries.com.

 My name is Kellie, and I am so thankful that I can share my testimony with all of you. As you read my testimony, I pray that you can see that you have a Heavenly Father who loves with a never-ending love. He cares so much and desires to walk in a relationship with you. You are a vessel He wants to use; you must give Him your yes.

I am no stranger to anxiety and depression. For years, anxiety and depression controlled every area of my life. Some days were more challenging than others. I remember the good days. I would soak in every second, but the good days were usually followed by some bad days or weeks. When COVID hit in 2020, it got awful. There were rarely any good days. Anxiety and depression consumed every area of my life. Daily activities were so challenging to do. I remember counting the hours until I could sleep because that was the only time I would get any relief. I kept this fight to myself because I didn't want anyone to know what I was going through. I didn't think anyone would understand, and I felt I needed to be strong for my husband and son. I didn't want to become a burden to them and didn't want them to know what was going on internally.

During this time, I managed to seclude myself from everyone, creating what I thought was a safe space where people wouldn't even notice what was happening to me. I also felt that if I didn't discuss what was happening to others, it might not exist. During this time, I believed so many lies about myself. I felt unworthy, unloved, alone, and like I didn't matter to anyone. The shame that I felt, though, was the worst part of it all. I knew I had so many reasons to be happy, but I couldn't be, no matter how hard I tried to do it alone.

In March 2020, I woke up one morning, and my first thought was I couldn't feel like this for another day. Thoughts of suicide began to race through my head. I remember feeling that everyone else would be better off without me and that I couldn't be anxious anymore. At that moment, I hit my knees in the middle of my living room and cried out to Jesus, my Savior. I just began to repeat the name of Jesus, and then I surrendered my life to Him. I can't even begin to explain the peace and love I felt at that moment. My tears changed from desperation to relief. I knew I wasn't alone any longer.

What lies do you believe from the enemy stealing your joy and peace? I want to encourage you to put some thought into this question. Once you have the answer, dive into Scripture and see who God says you are in Him. I still spend many hours in Scripture and prayer, asking the Holy Spirit to reveal my true identity in Him. I had always believed the lie that I had to clean myself up before coming to the Lord. Friends, that is so far from the truth. Scripture says that while we were still sinners, Christ died for us (Romans 5:8). You can come to Him just as you are, and He welcomes you with open arms. I want you to know that His love, peace, and grace are for you today.

The enemy likes to feed us with so many lies. He wants to steal our identity and overwhelm us with fear, anxiety, and shame so we will be distracted and led astray. The enemy's mission is to steal, kill, and destroy. But I have great news, friends! We have a Heavenly Father who loves us beyond measure. It is so important to get rooted in the Word of God and the truths that are in there about who God is and who we are in Him. God says you are dearly loved and chosen (1 Thessalonians 1:4), redeemed (Ephesians 1:7), more than conquerors (Romans 8:37), set free (Galatians 5:1). Don't believe the lie that these promises are not for you, because they are. God created you for a purpose; you are not here by accident or mistake.

KELLIE KIDNEY

Kellie lives in southwest Michigan with her husband, Brandon, and son, James. She loves being part of her local church and is passionate about women's ministry.

Kellie loves prayer, speaking, reading, and crafts. She is a Pepsi lover and Janice's bestie.

Kellie's favorite verses are Philippians 4:6-7:

Be anxious for nothing, but in everything by prayer and supplication, with thanksgiving, let your requests be made known to God; and the peace of God, which surpasses all understanding, will guard your hearts and minds through Christ Jesus.

What happens when our story doesn't look as we think it will? We can choose to give in to bitterness or trust God while waiting for His promises to come.

I've done both.

I have always desired and believed in God for a son. Years ago, in a prayer meeting, I remembered God's small voice saying, "I am going to bless you with a son." My husband, Jamie, and I were blessed with two beautiful girls, and I could not get pregnant as time passed. A good friend recommended that I see an endocrinologist, who confirmed that due to medical problems, my body was preventing me from pregnancy.

I was devastated. I questioned the promise God had spoken to my heart. I tried to re-interpret the promise and thought maybe He meant I'd have a grandson one day. The disappointment still weighed heavily on my heart, and I grew bitter. I struggled even to attend baby showers, so I didn't. That may not seem a big deal, but you're expected to go as a pastor's wife. I couldn't do it, and it caused my heart to break a billion more times than it already had.

I attended a Sunday morning prayer meeting at 227 (our church at the time, named after its address). I felt the weight of bitterness bogging me down so heavily. I begged God to take it from me because I was exhausted and did not want to feel the way I did anymore. I surrendered my will to God, and I felt a release within myself in that surrender.

Shortly after that, I was riding in the car with my husband and felt a "flutter" in my belly. I ignored it, thinking I must be going crazy. A few days later, I felt it again. Even though I felt like I was wasting my money, I bought a few pregnancy tests. Both confirmed that I was pregnant!

But I still didn't believe it.

My daughter had a physical around that time at the doctor's office, so I took the tests with me and had the doctor read them. He confirmed they read "pregnant." I was shocked and disbelieving that he offered to run bloodwork to confirm.

When he came in with the results, I saw his lips moving but heard nothing, just like you see in the movies. I asked him to repeat what he said, and he said, "you're going to have a baby."

When I got to the car with my daughter, still in complete shock, I asked her to confirm what the doctor said. She repeated that I was going to have a baby. I thought she must have misheard him, so I called the office. The doctor got on the phone and said, "Jill, you are going to have a baby!".

I scheduled an ultrasound, and what I thought would be a little peanut on the screen was instead a full-size baby! I was seven months pregnant with a little BOY! When the gender was announced, my husband and daughters were jumping up and down screaming. The room was so loud with celebration! I cried, thanking God for my miracle baby.

I waited fourteen years for the promise God had given me. Friend, if God has made a promise to you, He will always be faithful to fulfill it. Just keep praying. If God speaks, it doesn't matter. The timing may not look like you think, but if He spoke it, you could consider it done because He will never say a word that will become void. He keeps every promise He makes.

JILL GRISHAM

Jill is a fun-loving, coffee-drinking, southern woman full of charm and on a mission to share the love of Christ with other women. She is a force to be reckoned with as she follows God's call on her life with purpose and determination. She is selfless and gives herself freely, ready to serve where there is need, giving God her yes no matter the cost.

Jill has been in ministry with her husband, Pastor Jamie Grisham, for 17 years. They currently pastor Compassion Church in Dickson, TN, rapidly growing as they fulfill the call to reach the lost.

Jill profoundly connects with the Lord and enjoys her quiet moments with him. She loves spending quality time with family, especially her three children, Kaley, Abby, and River, who are God-given gifts and have blessed her life richly.

In 2018, Jill founded Compassion Women, which later became The Vine. The Vine is a flourishing women's ministry that seeks to empower women to walk in the freedom and purpose that comes with a close relationship with Jesus Christ.

God Can Do It Much Better.

Yeah, I grew up in the church. Sunday school lessons and the coloring sheets and all. Stamped with my auntie, aka the teacher's approval to take home and show momma just how good of a lil' "Christian" girl I was. I could rattle off the books of the Bible in order from front to back and had the ribbon to show for it. Our church was full of family; honestly, I looked forward to Sunday every week as a young lady.

When I reached my teenage years, I remember that's when I started to feel the Holy Spirit speaking to me. My friends and I got close in the youth group and could sense God in my life in a tangible way. One evening, I remember God asking me to give my life to Him. To completely surrender to Him. For some reason, I believed God didn't want me to have a life. I told Him, "But I want to have a husband and kids!" I told God "no" because I didn't believe He could give me the desires of my heart while also surrendering my life to Him. I thought I knew what was best for me.

I can say I have ALWAYS been a go-getter! If there is something I want, I would just put my mind to it and go after it! I pushed myself to the limits and always got what I wanted. Jobs, friends, moving, and, well, just STUFF! But I got to that point where I was ready to settle down. I wanted that family! So the second man who filled out the application got the job! Hired! He gave me a beautiful boy, but he also left me with a broken heart and a sweet baby boy to learn how to raise all alone.

You think that was getting me down? Nope, I was ready for some rebound love. Yep, you guessed it! I met another man who was much more fun this time, so I let my guard down. I was not going to stop until I got that family I always wanted. It was a whirlwind of spontaneity and chaos. At least this one didn't mind going to church here and there because I wasn't living for God, but I still knew exactly what I needed. This relationship was like a bad shipwreck movie sequel! The pain was so heavy trying to create this family I had always wanted so badly, but here I was with two sons I adored, yet I felt like such a failure.

The pattern kept going. No matter how hard I tried to give my boys a good family, I couldn't do it.

Fast forward thirteen years later, God's hand was on me this whole time. The enemy always wants us to believe God is withholding things from us. I wanted the family so badly, but I believed God didn't want that for me for some reason. It's like I thought He wanted me all to Himself but wouldn't give me the desires of my heart, and to be honest, I believe now that God is the One who put that desire in there, to begin with!

I have been married for seven years now. I have three amazing boys who are all so loved! Our family now is everything I ever wanted. God gave me the desires of my heart, but I couldn't ever be happy all those years ago because I believed in a big lie of the enemy!

Eight years ago, I found myself broken and defeated. I had the man and three awesome kids, but our life was a mess! God let me get to where I was finally at the end of myself. I cried out to God for many nights. I missed His friendship. I missed His love. I missed His guidance, but I couldn't be at peace with Him as long as I accomplished my dreams by my standards. I knew I needed Jesus. I cried out for Him, and He finally showed up. There's something about when you get real raw and cry out to the Lord, and I promise you, He shows up!

He began to turn my life around. He made Himself known to me and made me realize how He has been with me the whole time. He never left me. He waited patiently to realize I needed Him, but I missed Him more. What I had with Him growing up was extraordinary. His love was everything I ever really needed. His love was the very essence of what I was missing to be able to grow and nurture the family I always wanted.

You see, my love outside of God is nothing. I could only give scraps to my children and husband, but now I have resurrection life coursing through my veins. Not to say everything is perfect, but I can love and support and be there for my family now in ways that we can't do without God's Spirit breathing life into us each day.

The search is over when God steps in on the scene; that's it! He's all you need. He has taken what seemed like a broken family and turned it into a beautiful masterpiece. Though the master is still creating His work of art, I am so grateful to say that I have experienced the restorative and redemptive power of the blood of Jesus Christ and the power of the Holy Spirit at work in my life.

You're never too far to cry out to God! I can promise you; He's closer than you realize!

KRISSY CLOSSON

Hi! My name is Krissy Closson. I currently work at the world's greatest coffee shop ever! It's called Refuge Coffee House in Quincy, Michigan. I have three awesome sons, Demetrius, Blake, and Cooper, and the best husband ever, Steven! We moved to Michigan three years ago from the big ol' state of Texas, where I spent almost four years studying pastoral leadership at Southwestern Assemblies of God University! GO SAGU! My passion is to see God restore and redeem families and relationships to Him and on to wholeness. If He did it for me, He could do it for you.

The reality of my life is that God has stepped in to save me every single time.

I remember growing up and facing challenges; I doubted His love would save me. I thought the miracle child He gave my parents was a miracle for them, not me. My parents could not have a kid for eight years, and by the time I came along, it was impossible odds-but God beat them. I grew up hearing about my life with the title 'miracle child' attached to that, and honestly, it always made me feel less than adequate. I thought I didn't match up to the miraculous identity I'd been given. I began my journey in middle school with my identity and mental health challenges.

I began experiencing many external and internal changes that warped how I viewed myself and made me feel unworthy. My love for my life was taken away by the thoughts I had let control me, and in its place was a deep-rooted voice telling me there was no purpose for me. By thirteen, I had fully defined myself as someone who wouldn't make it till the following year. I struggled with self-harm and other addictions that caused me to fall further into despair. I was depressed and anxious; anxiety attacks and breakdowns controlled my life, and I fell behind in everything. I was truly at my lowest. I remained like that for a long time, but throughout every point, something stronger than me told me to keep going.

Then something miraculous happened, and I found peace. After years of living in a nightmare of drowning in my thoughts, I could breathe for a moment. With that small moment of peace, I was able to see Him. To realize that whatever was happening in my mind wasn't as suffocating as God's all-encompassing love for me. His love remained through it all. I found that at this moment, I wasn't just a miracle baby; I continue to be a miracle. It is unbelievable sometimes to think about how I am here today. The God that fought for my parents to have me continues to fight for me to be here. As I continue my adventure of a story, I realize every part is just an addition to the thousands of miracles that keep me here. His sacrifice is continued because people can read my story not from an obituary but as a testimony. The miracles and testimonies in my life stand out as who God remains to be, no matter how much we change. His love isn't limited to our thoughts or circumstances; it is simply a choice to let Him bring you peace in those situations. Have hope through your challenges, and let His peace and wisdom guide your heart.

LYDIA RODRIGUEZ

Lydia Rodriguez is a young woman with a heart for helping others and serving God through her gifts. She attends Holland First Assembly of God and is in her junior year at Holland Christian High School. Lydia enjoys spending time with her friends, writing, and reading.

Look Up, Woman of God!

My heart pounded through my chest as I stood patiently waiting for the guest speaker to pray for me. She was everything I wasn't. Her figure was tall and slender, her hair was shiny, and she had a stylish, confident vibe. My clothes were secondhand, my nails unmanicured, and my curly hair was fuzzy beyond submission, but my heart was yearning for more than the external. I stood in that line because I knew God was calling me forward.

My gaze never met hers. She took my chin and said, "Look at me, the woman of God! Look at me!" It took me forever to lock eyes with her. She told me that God would give me the confidence to look her in the eyes and at anything I faced from that moment forward. You see, I was afraid. I was afraid to lock eyes not only with who I truly was but also to overcome the enemy and to speak truth and life to others.

I let comparison cripple and steal from my life for way too long. If I didn't measure up, I tried to work harder or become someone else's "version of myself" to fit in. That didn't work, either. God doesn't make clones; He makes MASTERPIECES! One-of-a-kind creations to fulfill His purposes on earth! Ephesians 2:10 says, *"For we are His workmanship, created in Christ Jesus for good works, which God prepared beforehand that we should walk in them."* Our lives have a PURPOSE!

Comparison is an ugly disease. It rots your sense of self-worth and cripples your innovation. The antidote is to embrace your story and be authentically you. The Bible says comparing ourselves to others is unwise (2 Corinthians 10:12).

Today, if you are trying to "work" to be accepted or compromise who you are so that others will like you more, I invite you to learn from my story. Look up, the woman of God! Look into the eyes of Jesus! The One who made you and called you by name. The One who has anointed you for this moment in history to bring Him glory in your corner of the world.

God is asking you, "What is it that you can do?" We often look at the "cant's" and focus on what we don't have. We measure our lives by comparison. God will use you right where you're today, flaws and all, if you humble yourself before Him and give Him what you DO have. Give Him what you have because He is MORE THAN ENOUGH to fill in anything you may feel you lack. (Exodus 4:1-2)

Comparison is a thief. It steals the gift of "you." Every flower had to push through a dark place as a seed, a ton of dirt, and even that awkward stage where no bud could be seen. If God has called you, nothing can stop it, not even your insecurities!

Keep pressing forward! Keep looking up! God made you unique on PURPOSE!

ROSE RODRIGUEZ

Rose Rodriguez is passionate about seeing women achieve their God-given purpose and identity. She has been blessed to be Mrs. Michael Rodriguez for the past 23 years. Their lively, lovely teen daughter keeps them on their toes! Rose is also an ordained pastor at Holland First Assembly of God, where she leads the women's ministry, the "Holland First Ladies." In her free time, she loves spending time with friends and family and consignment shopping!

I had been struggling for a few months with boredom and a huge desire to stay home, especially after being home for so many weeks after my first surgery in February 2021. In June, my work computer began acting up, and there were some issues with it, and I was accused of going to websites that were not allowed and having sensitive information on my desktop. That night I was so upset I went to my room with my Bible, just started writing down verses for comfort, and prayed for God to take away the hurt and frustration. Although I proved that neither of these things I was accused of was true, they still stripped down my access to the point that I wasn't even given the ability to Google. I had two friends working remotely, and I just wanted to find a job where I, too, could work from home. Since my husband is an automotive technician, health insurance coverage has always been up to me, so not only did I want a remote job, it needed to have good health insurance and decent pay. I prayed boldly for God to move mountains, allowing that to come to me. As I continued to pray this same prayer, I started feeling like God was telling me He would move mountains for me.

At the end of June 2021, while we were on our way up for our annual Mackinac Island trip, my friend who works for the State of Michigan informed me of a job opening for the state that was also remote. As soon as we were checked into our hotel, I got on my laptop and applied immediately. Then it seemed like these remote job openings with the state were coming out of the woodwork! I applied for everyone for which I was qualified. God was sending so many opportunities my way! He was moving mountains! I had never before seen so many remote jobs become available, and since they were for the government, they included great pay and insurance!

After submitting applications for several positions, I finally received a call for an interview. And, because God is so amazing, it just happened to fall on a day during the week when I was coaching color guard for band camp, so I didn't have to come up with any weird excuses. The night before my interview, I prayed for confidence and strength. I looked up and wrote down 3 to 4 pages of Bible verses on strength and courage. On the way up to Lansing for the interview, I listened to worship music and prayed for God to go into that interview with me. I had never felt more comfortable and confident during an interview EVER! I believe that was a practice run since I didn't get contacted for that position. I did get another interview but found out that it wouldn't be remote for the first year, so I declined.

I continued applying for more remote jobs and praying. I had another foot surgery in August 2021 that kept me home for about three weeks. I spent that time developing a routine of Bible studies in the Bible app, watching an inspirational video on YouTube every morning, and doing a devotional in the afternoons. Just being home, I felt so at peace. Going outside, I breathed in the fresh air and felt God's presence. Sitting on the front porch doing my devotional was just so amazingly peaceful. The night before I returned to work, I woke in the middle of the night and had difficulty going back to sleep, so I prayed.

As I prayed, I felt powerful that I would get a call about that job that week. Well, it wasn't that job I had interviewed for; it was for another state job. They wanted to interview me that week. As I left work that first day back, I prayed to thank God for getting me through the day, and it dawned on me. This job that I was going to interview for is remote! This is precisely what I wanted! God can and will do much more than we can think or imagine. The interview went well. They said I'd find out either way by the following Friday. The next day after the interview, I discovered they had called all my professional references! Throughout this journey, parts of the two songs ran through my head. The words, "Not once has He ever stopped moving. Not once has He ever let go. Never has, never will. My God is still the same," as well as "Yes He has, and yes He can" had been playing on repeat in my mind over about a month or so.

I assumed I would get a phone call that Monday, but after not hearing anything all day, I started to have doubts. I also kept remembering God's promise and just having faith. That night I got that strong feeling again, telling me I would get a call the next day. Again, I can't explain how great God lines things up! My phone is set to 'do not disturb while I'm driving. Ironically that day, I had to go to the store after work. I would've usually been driving at this particular time, but as I was getting ready to leave the store, my phone rang, and it was the job offer! If I didn't go to the store, I wouldn't have gotten that phone call, and who knows how long that game of phone tag would've been.

I have always wondered how people hear God's voice, but I have slowly come to recognize it as an overwhelmingly strong feeling that accompanies specific thoughts.

November 1st, 2022, will mark my one-year anniversary with the State of Michigan, and it has been more wonderful than I can ever explain. My boss is an amazing God-fearing woman with whom I share several commonalities. My coworkers are the nicest, most understandable, and most incredible people I've ever worked with.

I was nervous after being in the same place for nearly ten years, but I also trusted that God completely controlled this fundamental change. I remember often thinking, 'I just want a job working from home with good pay and benefits.' But it seemed like an impossible dream. But, again, NOTHING is impossible with God!

AMY ABREY

Amy Abrey lives in Michigan with her husband, Michael, and daughter, Ashlyn. She also has an adult son, Zachary. Her passions include her faith, family, fur babies, and Disney.

In a world plagued by comparison and the pressure to prove yourself, being who God created you can be arduous and sometimes even scandalous.

I'm no stranger to the ploy of trying to play a part I was never created for. As young as second grade, I remember falling asleep on tear-stained pillows and begging God to change me. I vehemently detested almost everything about myself. I wouldn't say I liked the way I looked. I hated my personality. I hated that I was so loud, outgoing, and funny. I felt different from the other girls at school, and the desire to simulate was so strong, yet it felt impossible. Young hearts were not created for this crushing. I battled silent suffering within myself, a secret war that no one but I knew was being waged.

Because I didn't yet know the One Who created me, I allowed my irrational thoughts, the opinions of others, and blatant attacks of the enemy to create fabricated walls of insecurity in my heart and mind. These absurd walls were strongly fortified; one enemy lay upon another with each brick. The negative voices of others became mortar between the bricks, only serving to validate the lies I already believed about myself. "Not good enough" was the script I repeatedly rehearsed, and if I'd had an audience, I would have received a standing ovation for my perfectly articulated performance.

I was persistently persuaded of my value and worth by those around me and by what the media fed me. Being gauged by others who don't know their identity is damaging, and undoing that damage is only possible through Christ.

In my most vulnerable years, I had no shield or foundation of truth to wage war against the onslaught of relentless personal attacks. My responses typically looked like tears and angry outbursts. I was a very emotional child with no grasp on dealing with the roller coaster of emotions I often felt. I was hyper-sensitive to things as petty as facial expressions. Many family functions were marked with memories of me storming off in a rage or crying for no reason.

My solution for never feeling "good enough" became pressure to prove myself in other ways. Throughout my school years, I soared academically. In high school, I took classes with upper-level students and advanced placement classes within my grade level. My parents never had to remind me to do my homework. In band, I was always an upper chair for clarinet. I auditioned for a musical, got one of the lead roles, and was given a song solo.

Being academically bright is a gift, but it can easily become a faulty measure of self-worth and a form of idolatry. It was both for me. My validation came from good report cards, aced tests, and knowing I was advanced beyond my peers. When others achieved success, my natural response was not to celebrate them. My internal response was criticism and the belief that I could also accomplish what they did, probably even better if I tried.

Even through all of my academic accomplishments, nothing ever filled the void inside me. No amount of accolades, awards, or scholarships could validate me in the way that I needed. Applause for accomplishments is short-lived, and the need for the next achievement will keep you chasing the winds of validation in hopes of proving yourself worthy.

I discovered the true definition of approval when I encountered God and His incredible love as a late teen. I learned that my identity lies solely in the One who created me. He made me with my unique personality and gave me a loud laugh that I no longer try to hide. Loving God has helped me learn to love myself.

His Word has transformed me and renewed my mind (Romans 12:2). I realized He alone is my source of definition and validation, and I don't need approval from anyone outside Him. If people love me, that's great. If people don't, that's fine, too. I ultimately know He loves me with undying love and has set me free from the need for man's approval. Unraveling the spider web of untruths has been a journey, but one that I willingly yield myself to as He continually transforms me into the image of Himself (2 Corinthians 3:18).

JANICE RIGEL

Janice, AKA "everyone's BESTIE," is a joyful, laughter-loving girl with a passion for a faith-filled life. Her heart is to collide humor with the truth of God's Word to inspire others to fall more in love with Him.

Her desire is for all who have been silenced by the pains of life to have their voices restored and used to speak life and give hope to others in need of the same restoration.

Janice is the Podcast Host of 'Journey with Janice and Author of 'Slayin' Singlehood,' 'Come Away With Me' and several smaller devotionals. She is a Christian life coach and mentors many. She shares her story and biblical truth to encourage everyone to celebrate life in every season.

He Told Her Story

A woman frustrated and barren, teased and tormented, unable to get pregnant. Her greatest desire finally fulfilled. She bore a son.

Her name was Hannah.

He told her story.

A woman who broke all the rules, risking her life to save her people. She found favor with the king and spared them all.

Her name was Esther. He told her story.

A woman who lost her husband and left her homeland. She worked hard and married her kinsman redeemer. Her name was Ruth. He told her story.

A woman of divine influence. Known for her wisdom, courage, faith and action. She was a judge, warrior, prophet, poet, singer and songwriter. Without her leading, others wouldn't even enter the battlefield, and with bravery she led.

Her name was Deborah. He told her story.

A woman unmarried and pregnant, surrounded by criticism and a husband-to-be who almost canceled the wedding.

She carried and bore the Savior of the world.

Her name was Mary, the mother of Jesus. He told her story.

A woman possessed by 7 demons, completely set free by the power of Christ. She funded the ministry of Jesus, witnessed His crucifixion and was the first to see Him after the resurrection.

Her name was Mary Magdalene. He told her story.

A woman who liked to stay busy and is known for her rarity of rest. She served and waited on the Lord diligently, even through her frustrations.

Her name was Martha. He told her story.

A woman marred by a failed marriage, drowning in insecurity and heartsick with hope-deferred. She let the Lord heal her, redeem her story and use her to inspire and impact the nations. She is confident. She is bold. She is your bestie.

My name is Janice. This is my story.

Just like He tells my story and countless others throughout history, your story tells of Him, too. A God who knit you together perfectly in the womb of your mother and created you to do and be more than you can imagine. It tells of a God who is not distant, but desires to be known and near. A God like no other. Who delights in every detail of your life. Whose gaze is always toward you. Whose attention is always on you.

Whose very good thoughts toward you outnumber the sand of the sea. Who rejoices over you with singing. Whose banner over you is love. Who surrounds you with songs of deliverance. A God who is forever faithful, always for you and works all things together for good. A God who uses pain for purpose, destruction for destiny and your story for His glory.

He holds your story. He writes your story. He redeems your story.

So tell it.

ABOUT KHARIS PUBLISHING:

Kharis Publishing, an imprint of Kharis Media LLC, is a leading Christian and inspirational book publisher based in Aurora, Chicago metropolitan area, Illinois. Kharis' dual mission is to give voice to under-represented writers (including women and first-time authors) and equip orphans in developing countries with literacy tools. That is why, for each book sold, the publisher channels some of the proceeds into providing books and computers for orphanages in developing countries so that these kids may learn to read, dream, and grow. For a limited time, Kharis Publishing is accepting unsolicited queries for nonfiction (Christian, self-help, memoirs, business, health and wellness) from qualified leaders, professionals, pastors, and ministers. Learn more at:
https://kharispublishing.com/

CPSIA information can be obtained
at www.ICGtesting.com
Printed in the USA
JSHW050312141222
34855JS00004B/10